Mature Elegance:

Styles and Techniques for Mature Clients

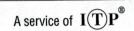

Mature Elegance:

Styles and Techniques for Mature Clients

by
LOUISE COTTER AND SARA RINGLER

Milady Publishing
(a division of Delmar Publishers)
3 Columbia Circle, P.O. Box 12519
Albany, New York 12212-2519

NOTICE TO THE READER

Cover Design: Kristina Almquist

Milady Staff
Publisher: Gordon Miller
Acquisitions Editor: Joseph Miranda
Project Editor: NancyJean Downey
Production Manager: Brian Yacur
Art/Design Production Coordinator: Suzanne Nelson

COPYRIGHT © 1998
Milady Publishing
(a division of Delmar Publishers)
an International Thomson Publishing company I(T)P®

Printed in the United States of America
Printed and distributed simultaneously in Canada

For more information, contact:
Milady/SalonOvations Publishing
3 Columbia Circle , Box 12519
Albany, New York   12212-2519

  2 3 4 5 6 7 8 9 10 XXX 03

Library of Congress Cataloging-in-Publication Data

Cotter, Louise.
    Mature elegance: styles and techniques for mature clients / Louise Cotter and Sara Ringler.
    p.   cm.
    ISBN: 1-56253-339-8
    1. Hairdressing. 2. Beauty culture. 3. Middle aged women. 4. Aged women. I. Ringler, Sara. II. Title
IN PROCESS   97-14863
646.7'24–dc21   CIP

646.724
Cot

53. 51

Contents

CHAPTER  **Hairstyling—Various**

Finishing Techniques 143

Preface

Mature Elegance is a book of style selections and helpful technical tips to assist you in targeting this important segment of society, and only mature models are shown, in a variety of adaptable forms and textures. Imagine how elated your mature clients will be that you put such value on their patronage!

Mature women are not only a large percentage of your business but are also powerful business executives and diversified professionals who provide a valuable exchange of ideas—and are ultimately your best means of advertising your services. They each have a need to look their very best at all times and are more than happy to refer you to their friends and colleagues.

Never underestimate the desire of a mature woman to look fashionably glamorous. Just keep in mind that while everyone wants to *grow* old no one wants to *look* old. You can be the catalyst that suspends "age" in limbo while catering to the unique beauty in each individual client.

Keep an illustrated book of styles just for this age group and constantly suggest updated versions of their favorite looks. Not everyone wants a change—they simply want an adaptable transition.

Introduction

The word *maturity* is bandied about in a myriad of ways. As it relates to society it is used most often as a reference to the number of years one has lived. As it broadly relates to the consumer, the interest turns sharply to market shares and percentages. Professional salon owners are acutely aware of the impact a mature clientele has on their business. Statistics indicate that clients between the ages of 55 and 65 make up almost half of the business in the average American salon.

A selective survey of mature clients of several Central Florida salons indicated that many, if not most, either had held or are still employed in high-profile positions. Most have two or more years of college or its equivalent. They are sophisticated, socially connected, and well informed. Clients of an age addressed in this text, when asked, indicated they prefer to frequent a professional salon that services a diversified age group but, however, definitely want to be treated as mature, feminine individuals and not as one of the young teenage crowd.

It is a fact that all Americans are aging. In 1980 the median age of Americans was 28. By the year 2000 more than half of the population will be over 40 years old. These so-called aging Americans are living longer, leading an active lifestyle, and staying in the workplace to an older age. Retirement has become an option, not a forced rule.

The word *mature* often has an implied stigma, when actually the literal meaning is quite beautiful. Consider some of these definitions as applied to your "55 or over" clients:

- Perfected by time or natural growth
- Ripe or ready to be put to action
- Ready for any special use
- A state of perfection or completeness

While maturity has many blessings it is not totally burden-free. "Life begins at 40" is a lovely and inspirational proverb, but certain things need to happen to encourage that new beginning. As a professional you become a key player in enhancing the potential beauty and well-being of your clients.

Every age has its own beauty, but in order to appreciate the beauty at hand one must let go the self-image of yesterday. That is much easier said than done. Most women who are 55 and over look back fondly at a particular year when they were the happiest, or felt the most glamorous. Often they mistakenly believe if they wear the same hairstyle and makeup they will look as they did at their youthful peak. In reality the opposite is true. A time-warped hairstyle will only make them look older. It is your responsibility, as a professional hairstylist, to steer her in the right direction.

In order to understand the needs of your mature clients a few interesting facts are fun to use as a reference. For instance:

A WOMAN OF 55

… was born in 1942 and was at her beauty peak (in her opinion) between 1952 and 1969. She was greatly influenced by Jackie Kennedy's impeccable style and elegance. She was, and probably is yet, fond of fitted sheaths and matching coats or short jackets, A-line dresses, and ultra simplicity. Her hair was more than likely worn in a midlength flip—exaggerated somewhat and held in place by back-combing and heavy holding spray. She likely still favors that look.

A WOMAN WHO IS 65 (OR OVER)

…was tremendously influenced by the introduction of television when TV celebrities became fashion role models. Crisp cotton shirtwaists for wearing at home (most women did not work), a voluminous chiffon skirt flowing from a fitted bodice, crinolines, circle skirts, and halter dresses were the look of the day. The hair was worn in short, fluffy bobs to look like Marilyn Monroe. This client may still have a "Monroe" mind-set.

The fact that fashion, at any time, takes inspiration from a former era tends to confuse some consumers when it comes to selecting a hairstyle that is adaptable and current. Extreme retro-fashion is best left to interpretation by the very young. Mature women seldom look their best in extremes of any kind. Everything should be done in moderation.

Style books in the reception area of most beauty salons feature hairstyles worn by youthful models. In the absence of realistic visual aids, mature clients are forced to ask their stylist to modify the styles shown. It is a real treat for the client who can browse through a picture book for the purpose of selecting a suitable hairstyle and relate to the models shown.

Finally, the hairstyle of a woman of any age, but particularly your mature client, should be determined by several important factors:

Body Size: Is she short, tall, thin, or overweight? Is her neck thick or thin, short or long? Are her shoulders squared or rounded?

Facial Features: Does she have excess fat on her face? Is her nose a little long or wide? Is her forehead low or high? Are her eyes set close together or far apart?

Personality: Is she full of life or vigor? Does she have a lighthearted disposition?

Career/Hobbies: Is she in business of any kind? How much spare time does she have to spend on hair care and personal grooming? Is she into sports, i.e., tennis or golf?

Mature Elegance is designed for your use in helping your clients meet their full beauty potential. While it's true that no two people are exactly alike, there is a common bond between women of mature age. They all want to look great. We hope that this book is a means to that end.

About the Authors

SARA RINGLER is a lifelong cosmetology professional. After completing a substantial formal education she elected to study the art of cosmetology. During her illustrious career she has experienced the admiration of her colleagues as a salon owner, educator, makeup artist, fashion director, and full-time participant in all facets of the beauty industry.

As a member of the Florida Cosmetology Association (FCA), FCA's Hall of Fame, the Florida Hair Fashion Committee, National Cosmetology Association's (NCA's) HairAmerica and NCA's EstheticsAmerica, she is in great demand as a guest educator and speaker at various industry functions. She has taught her artistic skills nationwide and beyond—to Canada and the Bahamas. As a makeup artist she counts among her clients numerous celebrities including George Hamilton, Florence Henderson, and former Miss America, Bess Myerson.

Ms. Ringler has served on numerous special education and administrative committees at local, state, and national levels, including NCA's prestigious Creative Design Committee, which is responsible for biannual trend and fashion releases.

Sara Ringler is a legend as the owner of multiple upscale beauty salons and co-owner of one of Central Florida's most reputable cosmetology schools. She and her equally talented husband, Woody, have for many years played a dominant role in the success of numerous salon professionals in Central Florida. She presently services the grooming needs of select clientele at Resultz, Inc., serves on the board of numerous community associations, and writes a health and beauty column for an NCA publication.

Ms. Ringler's professional skills have earned her the respect of her colleagues and loyal clients, many of whom are featured models in *Mature Elegance.*

LOUISE COTTER is a respected educator and leader in the cosmetology industry. Her dedication to the art of cosmetology is evidenced in her lifelong work as a salon owner, instructor, educational director, editor of a major industry magazine, and author of many educational texts.

Ms. Cotter's educational background provided the fundamentals necessary for communicating on multiple levels of cosmetology. In addition to a wide range of cosmetology skills, her professional expertise extends to art and journalism.

She is a licensed cosmetologist and cosmetology instructor who participates in industry-sponsored events, seminars, and continuing education programs nationwide. She is an accomplished platform artist and lecturer.

Ms. Cotter is also a member of the National Cosmetology Association (NCA). She received the first NCA Award of Achievement for excellence in cosmetology education. She is a member of the NCA Hall of Renown, Michigan Cosmetology Association's Hall of Fame, and the NCA Hall of Fame.

As director of education for a chain of cosmetology schools, she authored much of the supplemental material used in their educational system.

Ms. Cotter's contributions to the cosmetology industry and related education are numerous. She participated in the creation of many NCA Trend Releases and served two terms as OHFC/HairAmerica Style Director. She was trainer of the 1976 U.S.A. Ladies Olympic Hairstyling Team. Currently she is owner of Adrian Creative Images (ACI), a communications and media service company located in Central Florida.

Education and communication are her media; a love of the industry and a sincere wish to perpetuate excellence in cosmetology is her motivation.

CREDITS AND ACKNOWLEDGMENTS

Photographer: Sally Russ,
Winter Park, FL

Makeup: Leslie Ann Professional Beauty Services,
Orlando, FL

Hairstyles: Sara Ringler,
Styles by Sara, Resultz, Inc.
College Park, FL
Sherry Williams, Resultz, Inc.
College Park, FL

Face Lift product by
Mark Traynor, New York

Hair Enhancer product by
Jose Eber, California

Special Thanks to the following for contributions made directly or indirectly in
specific technical areas:
Leslie Ann—Central Florida
Pamela Taylor—New York
Veronica Garcia—California
NCA EstheticsAmerica Members
The Makeup Artists and Network Club Members—New York
NCA HairAmerica Members

Special Appreciation for the ladies who modeled for each technical presentation
and for their personal comments on the importance of physical appearance.

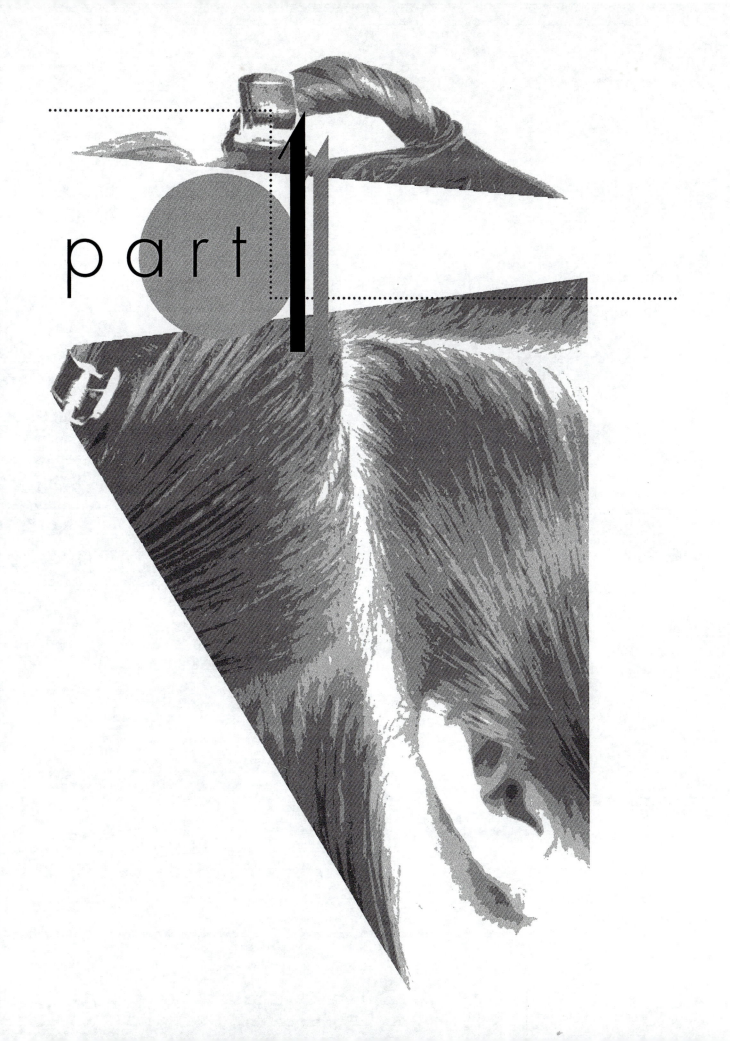

part 1

1

Marketing Salon Services to Seniors

diversification is a hedge against drastic changes in the economy and demographics

The average age of Americans is rapidly changing. It has been estimated by the American Association of Retired Persons (AARP) that approximately 12.7 percent of the population is over 65 and that figure will escalate as "baby boomers" hit retirement age.

Those figures are used as a marketing barometer by virtually every business nationwide, especially those offering personalized services. It stands to reason that as age groups change, so must your marketing strategy.

It is not considered the best business tactic to cater exclusively to one particular age group. As with financial portfolio, diversification is a hedge against drastic changes in the economy and demographics that have a direct bearing on your target clientele.

It is time now to recognize how valuable older clients can be to the stability of your salon. We in no way suggest that you "stack the deck." You already know that more than 12 percent of your potential clients are considered mature. Examine your books to determine what percentage of your regular clients fall into this category, then try to keep it at, or near, that count. If you walk into a restaurant and notice that most of the clients are seniors, you can count on the menu being regular fare, modest prices, and not an al dente vegetable in sight.

On the other hand, if the room is packed with teenagers, "gourmet hamburgers" will most likely top the food choices. The point is to know your clients, understand their likes and dislikes, and cater to their specific needs.

First, you may have to dispel some common myths held regarding older clients.

MYTH: Older clients are opposed to change.

FACT: Older clients are the ones who need salon services the most. They are not all conservative. Many aging ladies are eager for changes that will improve their physical appearance. Most shun extreme fads, believing the fads would be unsuitable for their facial features. Most often they are right. It is up to you to modify all extremes and let "adaptability" be your watchword.

MYTH: Senior clients only request traditional services (i.e., shampoo and set).

FACT: Many older clients would be receptive—even eager—for moderate change. It is doubtful that a client with beautiful white hair wants to become a Lucille Ball look-alike, but she would listen closely if her hairstylist suggested adding a bit of warmth to make her skin tone more vibrant and youthful looking.

MYTH: Creative excitement is missing when serving a 60-something client.

FACT: The mistake here is the risk of stereotyping any demographic group, and especially the "Golden Age" ladies. Indeed some of them are ultraconservative, while others are quite adventurous. As a young hairstylist you have not yet experienced the desperate feeling of aging and losing your beauty. Empathize just a bit and put yourself in their place. Just remember that most aging women (and men) have less hair than in their youth. They need every strand to frame their face in a flattering way. You can do a great service by suggesting subtle changes in their makeup techniques.

MYTH: Older women have given up on skin-care services, mistakenly believing it would not be beneficial.

FACT: Nothing could be farther from the truth! Women 55 and older spend the most money on over-the-counter skin care products, more than *any* other age group. What they may be wary of is the higher prices charged in some salons for fairly simple skin care services. The client is convinced they can do just as well by creating their own home-care regimen. They must be convinced that salon esthetic services are far superior to anything they can do at home. Remember: never make promises that you can't deliver. You are not a miracle worker. If a client's expectation is out of sync with real results, she is bound to blame you.

If a client's expectation is out of sync with real results, she is bound to blame you.

MYTH: Older clients don't purchase retail products from your salon.

FACT: A big misconception here. If they don't buy from you they will buy from any number of consumer outlets available to them. It is your responsibility to not only compare and stay in line with all available (over-the-counter) prices but to point out to your client that she receives professional help in selecting the proper product for her and that you are available for follow-up advice at no charge.

MYTH: Older, retired people are reluctant to spend money—in a word, cheap.

FACT: Simply not true. Don't be deceived by all the media hype about the disadvantage of living on a fixed income. Many older people are financially stable. They have planned carefully for a luxurious life after retirement and they are anxious to spend some of it on themselves…looking good…and having fun. They do make comparisons in price and quality of salon services, so be careful not to fall into the trap of raising prices without elevating services. They will simply not patronize your salon, but that doesn't mean they will not be spending their money elsewhere.

Mature women are astute shoppers. By years of experience they have learned to differentiate quality products and falsely promoted fast-marketing items. Remember: sell only quality products that you have tested and be sure each item produces the effect advertised.

While we know that respect must be earned, as a professional you have already earned a degree of respect. It is *confidence* you must earn. You can only do that by never promising the client more than you can deliver. Never build a client's expectations beyond reality. Remember always that a client is paying for your *time* as well as your talent. Give each individual your full attention while she is in your chair.

Mature clients are real treasures if you treat them as such.

CREATING AN INVITING ENVIRONMENT

The best way to find out exactly what pleases the 55-plus crowd is to ask them. Don't expect all women of that demographic age group to agree on everything, but our results showed that they came close when asked to describe the type beauty salon in which they are most comfortable. Listed are some of the most important points made by those we surveyed.

They were each asked the same question. And here are some of their answers.

What are the first things you look for when selecting a beauty salon? (Listed in the order of importance.)

- A well-appointed, color-coordinated reception area

- Fresh flowers or live, healthy-looking plants

- Well-organized reading material that is current and fashion-oriented

- A refreshing, subtle aroma of a floral/spice and herbal mix. A fragrance designed to induce pleasant relaxation

- Soft background music, preferably instrumental classics

- A well-organized reception desk staffed by a well-groomed, pleasant receptionist who greets me as if she is sincerely glad to see me…

- To be taken on time. If there is a waiting period I want to be told exactly how long I must wait and for what reason.

- I don't mind putting on a smock while I wait, but once I have undressed I don't want to sit in the reception area.

- If it is my first visit to the salon, I expect to meet and consult with the designer before my hair is shampooed.

- I expect to have the undivided attention of the stylist to whom I am appointed…nothing bothers me more than salon employees who converse with one another in the presence of a client. I feel that I am paying for his or her time and expect to receive good value for the fee.

- I want a designer to listen carefully while I describe the way I want my hair cut and styled instead of cutting me short by saying, "I know just what you mean," then give me whatever he or she pleases.

- I prefer small talk kept to a minimum and the topic never to be of a personal nature. My personal life is no one's business but mine and I am not interested in hearing anything personal about the stylist.

- I want to be informed about the products being used on my hair, but I dislike the feeling that I am being pressured to buy.

- I appreciate a salon staff that makes an effort to call me by name…especially after the first visit.

- I expect professional services given by first-class professional cosmetologists. If the services are no better than I can do myself, I have no interest in making a second appointment.

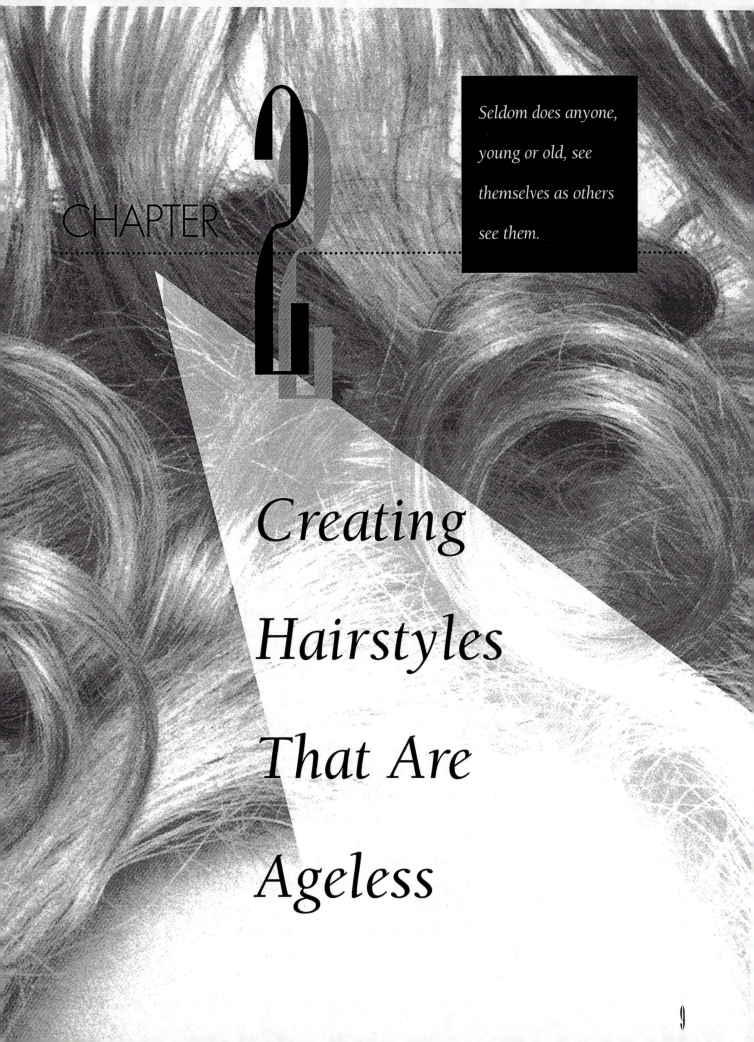

CHAPTER

2

Seldom does anyone, young or old, see themselves as others see them.

Creating Hairstyles That Are Ageless

The effect of a hairstyle should be free and the hair should look soft and touchable.

Women who are 55 or older need help from a professional hairstylist to design a form that will accentuate positive facial features and camouflage those that are less than perfect. Actually, the word *perfect* is a misnomer when describing a human face at any age. (And the older one gets, the less perfect the facial features become.)

By the time they have reached the golden age of 50 plus, most women have arrived at a length and a style that, right or wrong, they have adopted as their own. Some are locked into a particular time warp and are in no mood for a drastic change. Fortunately, a talented hairstylist can simply do a variation of the client's preferred look and bring her into a modern form that flatters her features as they are now, not as they once were.

Seldom does anyone, young or old, see themselves as others see them. While you are suggesting a subtle change to this very sensitive client, you will gain no favor by pointing out the features you seek to camouflage. Instead tell her which of her features are her best and design a style to focus on that asset. It is perfectly proper, however, for you to point out that as a woman ages, she should strive for a slightly new "feeling" in her hairstyle that works well with current fashion.

Older women tend to believe they should wear their hair short (and curly). That is a misconception, probably perpetuated by hairstylists lacking the imagination or skill to properly analyze and design for unique facial proportions. Actually, the hair can be worn any length depending on the body size and facial features. It is the line and form of the style that is important—the most flattering will be one that lifts her features.

Because many women 55 and older are career types they have already discovered that hair, makeup, and fashion work together, most are eager for your professional suggestions. It is up to you to use your expertise to soften even the most up-to-date trends to create an ageless look that incorporates what's new with a look that works uniquely for her.

Two mistakes that competent hairstylists avoid are unnatural colors and hairstyles that are too stiff. Both are telltale signs of women who are still stuck in their own time warp. If you execute an outdated style, you are catering to their reluctance to adopt a currently fashionable look.

Hair that is combed until every strand is rigidly in place, then sprayed to stay that way, no longer looks stylish or youthful. In fact it adds years rather than detracts. The effect of a hairstyle should be free and the hair should look soft and touchable.

Keep in mind that cut and color go hand in hand. Most people have varying degrees of gray by the time they are 40. The old saying that nature provides gray hair to soften one's features as they age just doesn't hold up these days. While some women may opt to keep their gray hair it doesn't mean they wouldn't look years younger with a great color to complement the skin tone and put a sparkle in their eye.

Never try to unduly influence your client to accept your suggestions pertaining to the color or haircut you believe would flatter her most. Simply state your professional opinion and hope she has enough confidence in your professional expertise to accept your advice.

To determine a client's best look, several factors must be considered before you cut a strand:

Thickness and texture must be considered first and foremost. Often as a person grows older the hair does strange, unnatural things. When the hair begins to turn gray the texture may change as well. Often graying hair becomes thin and unruly or less pliable. It depends entirely on the amount and the quality of hair you have to work with as to what hairstyle you can successfully create.

Balancing the facial features is very important. While you may use the rule of making all faces look oval for your younger clients, that rule is hard to follow once the features have taken on some signs of aging. Face shape in relation to hairstyle should be viewed differently for a mature person. Instead of trying to make everything a perfect oval, try to create a focal point by emphasizing the best facial qualities. Then examine the bone structure to see exactly what needs correcting. Consider a few basic facts:

Often graying hair becomes thin and unruly or less pliable.

- ❧ A round face may need straighter lines to give length. Curls would only tend to make it look even more round.
- ❧ An angular face can be softened by soft waves or curls.

Visualize the overall effect. It is a never-changing fact that the hair form (length and width) must balance the height and body type. A tall, lanky person does not look good in a closely cropped hairstyle. A small head form is not in harmony with a large, fleshy body. The same is true of long, voluminous hair on a petite body. It simply overwhelms all other attributes.

Take in consideration the amount of time one has to maintain her own hairstyle. For instance, does her hair require wet setting or can she go from wet to dry without rollers? How well can she handle a blow-dryer? Busy career women need easy-maintenance hairstyles.

Consider her lifestyle. Does she go to work each day? Does her job or professional position require a certain personal appearance? Even if the answer to both questions is yes, the hairstyle need not be simple to the point of being boring. She can be made to look special by giving her a haircut, supported by a perm if necessary, that will look terrific even when windblown or tousled. Again, it is the form that counts.

Design a hairstyle that is balanced so it can be combed in different ways for versatility and can be attractively rearranged for formal wear.

You should keep in mind that any hairstyle that is too structured also tends to harden the facial features. There is a fine line between an attractively "free" hairstyle and one that is aging and matronly. Strong lines are not flattering to most women at this stage of their lives.

HAIRSTYLES TO FLATTER FACIAL FEATURES

A hairstyle that is properly adapted to an individual not only emphasizes good facial features, but can minimize, or make less noticeable, the bad ones. Cosmetologists, not being cosmetic surgeons, must rely on creating an illusion by the form, volume, and detail of a hairstyle. As a person ages many less-than-desirable changes inevitably occur in the facial features. Most can be attractively camouflaged. What you should strive to do is create an overall effect that will delight your client and bring compliments from her friends. Remember: It is the total image that is seen when you meet someone for the first time.

Women go to cosmetology professionals because they want to look the best they possibly can. If they didn't have pride in their appearance they would simply dress their own hair. One noted hair designer and successful salon owner, when asked why his clients were all older ladies, answered without hesitation: "They are the ones who need me most."

Listed are a few of the most-common facial flaws that can be made less prominent by a flattering hairstyle.

Deep horizontal lines in the forehead

Fig. 2-1

- Most older women do not look their potential best with full bangs. There are exceptions, but most often too much hair on the forehead only accentuates the very problem you intend to hide.

- Create a softly feathered bang. If that still appears too heavy, pull wispy strands of hair onto the forehead for a newer, lighter look.

Small lines (crow's-feet) at the corner of the eyes

Fig. 2-2

- Avoid a style that has straight lines pulled away from the face at the temple area. Existing lines will only be exaggerated.
- Short, curled hair across the forehead and covering the receding areas tends to detract from lines around the eyes. The softness provides movement and interest that focuses on the hair instead of the little lines at the corner of each eye.

A sagging jaw line (jowls)

Fig. 2-3

- Hair that is short and tailored at the nape will accentuate any facial fullness. Avoid a style that follows the head form too closely in the temple area. By contrast, it may give the overall effect of a pearshape making the jowls look even larger.
- The hair above mid-ear level should be medium short with volume that is wider than the jowl protrusion. However, the neckline should be lengthened to draw attention away from the jaw. A form that cinches at the ears then shows hair peeking from the back below the earlobes is best for camouflaging a sagging jawline. The look will be even more effective with a soft perm that provides soft movement throughout.

A prominent nose

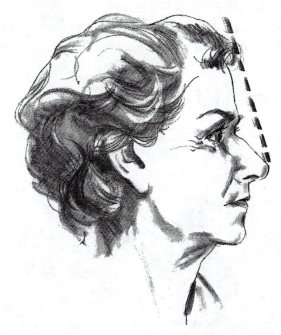

Fig. 2-4

> As a person ages, the bone structure does not change but the muscles and tissue surrounding the bone become relaxed. The nose seems to protrude and often droops a bit at the end. It is a mistake to pull the hair completely away from the face. Straight hair that lays flat against the head form is apt to accentuate a prominent nose.

> An asymmetrical form that frames the face with soft waves and adaptable volume will cause the nose to be absorbed into the total look.

A receding or protruding chin

Fig. 2-5

- A short hairstyle with all the volume above the ears will expose a less-than-perfect chin in a very unflattering way.

- Observe the client's profile. Balance the facial features with a hairstyle having volume and fullness in the front and a length no longer than the jawbone.

Large ears (wrinkled earlobes)

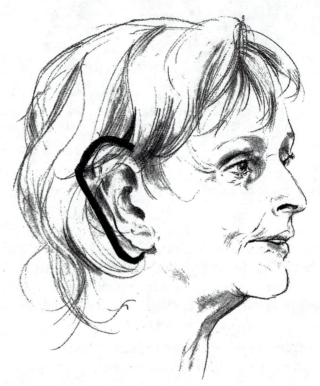

Fig. 2-6

- Some beauty experts say you can tell a women's age by looking at her earlobes. As if aging was not a sufficient problem, the ears seem to become enlarged and the lobes lose the fatty tissue. This results in wrinkled lobes.

- Cut the hair into a softly layered bob that slightly covers the earlobes. Feather the hair over the ears, being careful not to make it look heavy as if there was something to hide. Just a few hairs forward will even cover scars from a face-lift or a hearing aid.

A thin (or bony) face

Fig. 2-7

- The face can be likened to a treasured painting—and the hair should be a complementary frame. Balance and proportion are key words. Stay away from straight lines and excess volume.

- Hair that is layered throughout can be styled with the right amount of fullness to balance gaunt facial features. Allow soft, feathery strands to spill onto the forehead and temples.

A full, fleshy face

Fig. 2-8

- Depending on the size of the face as related to the body, the height of the hair in front should not extend a distance from the head that exceeds the distance between the eyebrows and the top of the natural head form. There should be little or no width below the top of the ears.

- Keep the sides close to the head while creating movement and adaptable fullness in the top. This form will pull facial lines upward without adding width.

Deep folds from the nose to the mouth

Fig. 2-9

- A hairstyle that covers too much of the face tends to draw attention to the deep grooves planted prominently in the center of the face.

- Design a style that exposes the face. A waved front with adaptable volume will draw attention away from those creases. An updo looks great in most instances.

A wide, short neck

Fig. 2-10

- A person that has no visible neck should never wear long hair unless it is arranged into an updo.

- Cut the hair just below the natural hair growth at the nape. The hair can be subtly graduated at the nape but care should be taken not to make it too fitted or shingled up the back.

Stooped shoulders

Fig. 2-11

- This is another instance when the head and body form should be viewed from a profile. By all means do not give this person a petite hairstyle. She has a tendency to carry her head forward of her shoulders. A small head will accentuate the humped shoulders.

- Create a hairstyle with fullness in the back. This balances, somewhat, the protruding shoulders.

CHAPTER **3**

Often the hair
becomes thinner
with age.

How Texture Relates to Adaptability

most older women look best with soft movement in the hair

As a person reaches middle age and beyond, the skin on the scalp undergoes changes, just as does the skin on the face and the rest of the body. It is not clear whether the bones in the skull actually shrink as one ages or the scalp just begins to tighten or loosen. In either case, as the scalp changes the hair follicles are affected as well. Hair that was naturally curly in one's youth may suddenly begin to straighten. This only means the follicle has changed its shape from oval to round.

Women who never needed a perm may desperately need chemical support after 55 just to control their hairstyle. Older women are less inclined to spend as much time blow-drying and arranging their hair as younger ladies do. They may ask for a short haircut and a tighter curl than they would have wanted at one time. However, this does not mean they want to emerge from a perm service looking as if they are wearing a scouring pad on their head. There is a happy medium between hair that is too tightly curled and hair that is loosely waved.

It is an accepted fact that most older women look best with soft movement in the hair. It is also a fact that a tight perm (small ringlet curls) adds age and detracts from their natural beauty potential.

Often the hair becomes thinner with age. It is possible—even probable—as the hair turns gray (loses natural pigment) it either becomes exceptionally fine and flyaway or wiry and unruly. Neither texture is ideal and your clients will expect you to make whatever correction possible.

To give your client texture and movement, start by wrapping the hair on perm rods having medium diameters. Use mild perm solution and carefully condition the hair after the chemical process. If the look is great, stay with the same procedure in the future. If you find that more or less movement or curl lends the greatest adaptability, adjust the rod size (smaller or larger) to attain the exact amount of desired texture. You may also alternate medium rods with small rods for a softer-but-firm effect. These techniques will give the client the best possible results.

Make no mistake about it—your client's best hairstyle depends on three factors: cut, that controls the form; texture, that supports the form and provides durability; and hair color, that makes the skin tone look lively and puts a sparkle in the eyes. It all adds up to adaptability.

Each step-by-step perm technique that appears in this book was selected and executed for the person shown wearing the style. Even though it takes a little longer, you should give a test perm curl before perming a first-time client. After the hair has been cleansed and properly prepared for perming, wrap three rods somewhere in the back of the head. Make each rod a different diameter to determine the exact amount of curl necessary. Apply perm solution and process 100 percent just as you would a regular perm. You can tell immediately which of the rods give the desired amount of texture for the finished style.

When you are putting chemical texture into a client's hair it is wise to leave the hair just a little longer than it will be worn until it has been permed. Then, cut the hair to the exact length and style desired. If the hair is cut short on top and even shorter in the nape, you are forced to reduce the diameter of the rods in the perimeter so the hair will make a minimum of one and one half turns around the rod. As a result, there may be more curl around the hairline than is needed for the style the two of you selected in your initial consultation. The result may disappoint both you and the client.

If you have any doubt that texture is a vital factor in individual adaptability, try a few wigs on your client. Make one very curly, one elongated waves, and one straight. It is a visual experience that instantly proves your point and helps your client make the right decision. Some salons have an imaging machine which, through the magic of a computer, allows the client to view herself in may different hairstyles. Any method that creates a mutual understanding between you and your client is the right way to go.

CHAPTER 4

Beauty is said to be in the eyes of the beholder.

Who Needs Haircolor and What Kind?

Haircolor can actually improve the condition of some types of hair.

Whether or not a woman really "needs" haircolor is debatable. It depends largely on her personal self-image, attitude toward fashion, how competitive she is forced to be in the workplace, and her lifestyle in general.

Beauty is said to be in the eyes of the beholder. If that is true, how she sees herself is the determining factor. Once a woman's hair starts to turn gray, she not only looks older but she feels older. It is a frightening time for most women and your clients need your help.

While your client may not want a drastic change in her appearance most women want to hold back the look of aging as long as possible. One, allover color may look harsh and unnatural. In-the-know professional colorists very often opt for a selective coloring technique instead. The colorist works with only a few strands here and there to frame the face unobtrusively with light and dark highlights.

If the hair is more than 20 percent gray it is a great opportunity to bleach strands throughout and cover the entire head with no-peroxide, no-ammonia color tone.

Haircolor can actually improve the condition of some types of hair. Often it adds body to fine, thinning hair. The greatest objection heard from clients is the necessary upkeep. They are reluctant to return to the salon every few weeks for a touch-up as the natural roots begin to appear. That objection can be overcome by offering one of many off-the-scalp hair coloring techniques.

Selective strands can be foiled and highlighted and the natural root will not show for months. Another factor that makes off-the-scalp coloring so popular is the versatility depending on how many hair strands are selected for a color change. When a lot of hair is foiled, it almost gives the appearance of a solid color, except that it looks more natural.

Every professional haircolorist has a list of tips on haircolor that he or she follows carefully. A few such tips are listed below.

THINGS TO REMEMBER WHEN COLORING A CLIENT'S HAIR:

- Pigment contained in the hair and skin are closely related; both fade as a person ages.

- It is a mistake to try to duplicate the hair color of a person when she was many years younger. It is more natural looking to make a brunette a few shades lighter than she was in her teens. Make natural blondes less bright.

- Medium contrast between skin tone and hair color is more flattering. Seldom does a natural blonde look good as a raven-haired brunette. Select the blonde tone that enhances her own skin tone.

- Natural redheads seldom look good as a blonde. Instead of bleaching the hair, try frosting or highlights a few shades lighter than the natural color.

- All off-the-scalp coloring techniques—frosting, highlighting or tipping—require minimal maintenance, possibly a touch-up two or four times a year.

- If you allow your client to select a color from a manufacturer's color chart, keep in mind those colors are as they appear on white hair. Your client will be disappointed unless you explain to her the difficulty of achieving that same color on her existing hair color.

- Snip off a few strands of the client's hair from somewhere underneath and color it with the product you have selected. Keep in mind, however, that the strands will respond differently off the head than they would if given the advantage of body heat while processing.

- Because the hair of African Americans is usually very absorbent, nonpenetrating hair colors work best. Select a product that has no peroxide or ammonia, one that will only penetrate the cuticle and add subtle color and shine to dark hair.

CLOSING A SALE WITHOUT ACTUALLY SELLING

All off-the-scalp coloring techniques require minimal maintenance.

You should present the advantages of change in hair color in a way that will make your client eager for the service.

Never give a client a false expectation. Use your professional knowledge to explain all the possibilities. If she has an unrealistic idea of the results she may not be at all satisfied in the end. Be sure you do not promise results that you cannot deliver.

The first rule for selecting the proper hair color for graying hair is to analyze the skin tone and the nature of the *existing* hair color, not the hair color that may have been at a younger age. Below is a simple chart suggesting a few basic colors to use on various shades of gray. Keep in mind that these may vary depending on texture and condition of your client's hair.

Skin Tone	Hair Color	Graying	Suggested Color Correction
Olive (green)	Black	20%+	Medium ash-brown tones for gray
	Dark Brown	30%	Slightly deeper than natural
	Blonde	10%+	Toned shades of ash blonde
	Red	Fading	Toned-down natural color range
Sallow (yellow)	Black	20%+	Warm auburn/dark golden browns
	Dark Brown	30%+	Maintain natural color/blend gray by highlighting
	Blonde	10%+	Light and dark high/low lights, overall ash tones
	Red	10%+ Fade	Blend gray with subtle red tones
Ruddy (pink)	Black/Dark Brown	20%+	Lighten hair to golden brown
	Light Brown	30%	Blend to golden brown
	Blonde	10%+	Blend gray to natural shade with semi-permanent golden blonde
	Red	20%+ Fade	Natural red tones/semi-permanent blend
Neutral (beige)	Black	20%+	Enrich gray with warm brown tones
	Light Brown	30%	Highlight and blend with golden tones
	Blonde	20%+	Lighten hair two levels using beige tones
	Red	20%	Blend gray to natural red tones and intensify the red with semi-permanent tint

Most professional haircolorists prefer to camouflage gray hair as opposed to covering it. They prefer to stay within the natural color range as well. Tones that lighten and brighten are preferred over colors that tend to drab the existing gray.

The best reason to color a client's hair is to make her look better in the most effective way possible. A simple consultation should be made with the client to advise her of the frequency of color visits that will be necessary. Then she will be comfortable and willing to provide the time to maintain her color.

Keep in mind that a satisfied color client is a loyal client forever.

CHAPTER 5

Cleanliness and sufficient moisture is of utmost importance.

Corrective Makeup for the Mature Face

Many share the same facial problems as they grow older.

Before instructing your clients on personal makeup techniques impress on them the importance of perpetual skin care.

Cleanliness and sufficient moisture is of utmost importance, especially for aging skin.

Recommend a deep-cleansing lotion or cream for removing all traces of old makeup, followed by a gentle scrub to remove remaining residue from the pores and exfoliate dead cells that form naturally on even the smoothest skin.

Follow the cleansing routine (morning and night) with a smoothing toner to firm the skin and close the pores. To replenish moisture lost in the cleansing process, recommend a light, greaseless moisturizer to help reduce the appearance of fine lines and wrinkles. A product containing SPF15, a level recommended by many dermatologists to help protect against UV rays, is desirable for skin of all types.

In addition to a regular skin care maintenance routine that the client does at home, urge her to book a monthly in-salon facial for the purpose of deep pore cleansing and additional nourishing nutrients.

PERFECTING IMPERFECTIONS

Forget the word "perfection." Everyone has *im*perfections that are impossible to hide, so why not make the most of that unique difference? No two faces are alike, but many share the same facial problems as they grow older. Here are some suggested makeup tricks to pass along to your clients.

Broken capillaries

Most small, but visible, broken blood vessels can be covered by using concealer under sheer foundation. Prominent scars may require a heavier, opaque makeup especially formulated to camouflage serious skin problems.

Wrinkled (crepey) eyelids

Because the skin of the eyelid is inclined to lose elasticity long before the rest of the face begins to show any signs of aging, it is a problem that must be dealt with. Use frosted, shiny, or pearlized eye shadows *only under the eyebrow area.* Over the eyelids use subtle shades of matte eye colors such as neutral, taupe, gray, brown, beige, burnt orange, dark olive green, mahogany, and charcoal. Apply with a small sponge stick using a small amount of color for the application.

Wrinkles at the corners of the eyes (crow's-feet)

Often makeup meant to conceal these tiny lines only emphasizes the problem by causing the skin to crack and crease. First, soften the skin around and over the eye with a rich moisturizer applied after the face is cleansed. Allow to remain for several minutes. Blot off excess moisturizer and apply foundation with a sponge and blot to achieve a sheer look.

Drooping nose tip

Use a light brown eye shadow and a sponge-tip applicator. Apply to the very tip of the nose after foundation and face powder have been applied and allowed to set for a few minutes. Blend well with the fingertips and make certain it is not noticeable.

Fleshy cheeks (jowls)

Use a special contour brush having short, angled bristles to apply light brown contour powder to the lower cheek area from the earlobe to the center of the chin. Blend well with a cotton ball until it is a faint shadow. Then brush with translucent face powder.

Creases/lines around the upper lip

First apply foundation, then outline and design the shape of the lips with a sharp lip liner the same shade as the lip color. Apply lip color with a lip brush then use a cotton swab dipped in face powder to pat onto the lip liner. Reapply lip color then blot gently. A small dot of sheer gloss on the lower lip will add shine.

Nasolabial folds (lines from the nose to the mouth)

Apply a lighter shade of concealer cream, with a very fine, light brush, into the area of the deepest creases. Blot lightly and recover with foundation, then blot and dust with powder.

Undereye pouches

Soak tea bags in ice water; squeeze excess water and hold over the eyes a few minutes to reduce any swelling. Use an eyeliner brush to apply concealer into the darkest part of the sunken areas that surround the pouch. Pat gently using no pressure to blend the concealer. Make certain to keep the concealer confined to the indented areas. Allow to set for a few minutes then apply sheer foundation over the entire area.

Faded skin tones

It is not unusual for the skin to lose pigment as one ages. Select a fresh, clear color blush such as coral, rose, or apricot in powder form. Apply color with a blusher brush to the cheekbone and sweep it up toward the hairline. Curve the color softly around the temple. A sweep of the brush just under the jawbone from ear to ear can be very effective for giving the facial features a special glow. Use a clean, dry sponge wedge to blend the blush.

Most mature clients need help with their makeup regimen. Make an appointment to give them a complete makeup lesson. Help them select the appropriate colors and makeup items necessary, then instruct them as they make the application. It's important that each person knows how to apply her own makeup to her best advantage. She only has one face on which to practice until she perfects her own individual routine.

MAKEUP TIPS FOR MATURE CLIENTS

Perhaps the most important message regarding makeup for your mature client is "use a light touch." Harsh colors and trendy techniques will detract from the natural beauty of most mature women.

Make it a habit to prepare a monthly beauty bulletin to hand out to your clients when they visit your salon. It may prove to be one of your best marketing tools. Here are a few application tips for you and your mature clients:

- Create a well-arched brow with absolutely no straggly hairs. The brow actually sets the facial expression and lifts all other features.

- Keep in mind that foundation should not be used as a total cover-up. Instead it should be used only to even out the skin tones. The foundation should be ultratranslucent.

- Mature faces look best in warm tones, such as peach and coral, as opposed to pink or red. Be sure to complete a skin and hair color analysis to ensure correct tones.

- Use gray or brown eyeliner instead of black and switch to a blush having a coral base.

- Use extra-fine face powder that will not collect in the tiny lines or creases that inevitably appear in aging faces.

- Apply lip primer to the lips to avoid color seeping into unsightly feathery cracks on the upper lip. Then line and fill the lips with a lip pencil followed by a sheer lip color.

- Natural skin tone and hair color basically determine the makeup palette most adaptable to an individual.

MAKEUP TECHNIQUE—CUSTOM DESIGNED

As a woman ages, she faces the challenge of updating her usual way of applying makeup. The same techniques used on her younger face simply no longer work, although she falls into a habit through the years of doing her hair and makeup the same way. Once, when her skin was firm and every feature youthful, her heavy-handed makeup application was great. Now she needs a lighter hand and some deemphasizing instructions from a professional.

You serve the client's best interest by playing the role of an instructor. The object is to teach her how to apply her own makeup to camouflage the inevitable signs of aging and give the face a natural glow.

Instruct your client to always apply her makeup in real daylight if possible. If not, then light the room with daylight-like bulbs. The light that falls on the face should be evenly balanced and never from one source above the head. The entire face should be free of shadows.

Use a large magnifying mirror so every detail can be seen. Set aside sufficient time for the application so you are not tempted to take shortcuts on some of the application steps.

Of equal importance is the correct color selection. Your client needs your guidance step-by-step to get her started:

1. Consultation and color selection.
2. One makeup session that you apply while explaining in detail the reason and application technique.
3. Selling the client the proper application brushes, sponges, and so on.
4. Observing while the client does her own application following your instructions.

Fig. 5-1 Before: A makeup
application is much
like creating a
beautiful painting—
you must start with a
clean canvas. All
mature skin needs a
touch of moisture.
Apply a moisturizer
and allow it a few
minutes to absorb
before starting to
apply the makeup.

Fig. 5-1A After

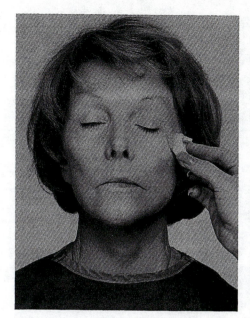

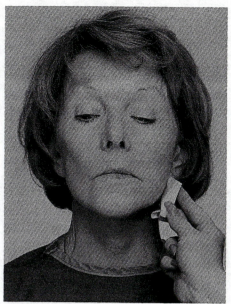

Fig. 5-2   Use a small triangular sponge to apply concealer under the eyes and to mask any age spots or blemishes.

Fig. 5-3   Apply foundation (a color that closely matches the natural skin tone). Use a damp sponge for sheer coverage and stroke the foundation *downward*.

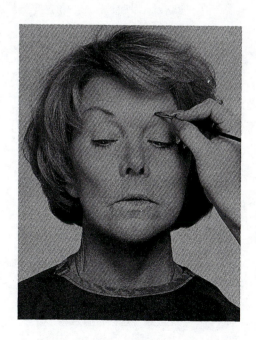

Fig. 5-4   Fill in the natural brow line with an angled contour brush. Use a soft shade of muted light brown or gray for the most natural look.

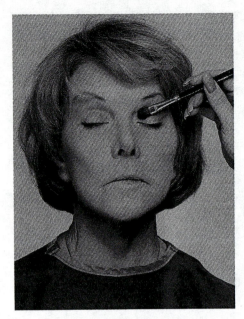

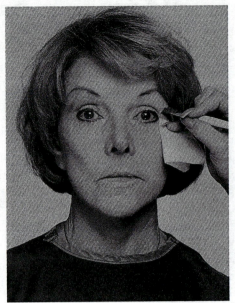

Fig. 5-5 Apply a warm color to the crease of the eyelid just under the brow line. If the eyes are deep set a lighter shade should be used so the eyes do not appear to recede. Line the outside rim of the eye with an eyeliner pencil.

Fig. 5-6 Hold a tissue under the eye as protection from falling powder while you apply finishing highlights to the eyelid. Apply a soft brown mascara to the upper and lower lashes.

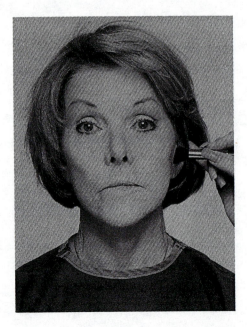

Fig. 5-7 Apply cheek color just under the cheekbone, extending from the temple to the center of the eye.

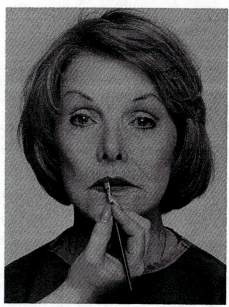

Fig. 5-8   Outline the lips with a pencil   Fig. 5-9   Use the same color to fill in
            or a narrow lip brush.   the lips and build up the
                                                          upper lip as needed.

Fig. 5-10   The face should look
            soft and natural.

The following tips passed on to your client will help her achieve the desired
results:

1. Use sheer foundation to even out the skin tone, not to hide flaws.
2. Use the color tones most complementary to the skin and hair.
3. Avoid black eyeliner, use brown or gray.
4. Before applying lip liner or color use a lip primer to avoid feathering in
   the creases of the upper lip.

THE LIFT—A TEMPORARY, NONSURGICAL FACE-LIFT

For a special occasion or a photo session the "Lift" is a great way to give the face a smooth, youthful appearance.

The Lift is widely used by makeup artists who specialize in the field of entertainment, such as movies and television. It can be used by both men and women, but a wig must be worn if the natural hair is too short to hide the elastic bands that hold adhesive strips in place.

The Lift was created by noted makeup artist Mark Traynor who, after a long illustrious career, still manufactures and markets various beauty aids including a full line of stage and consumer makeup. The Lift is simple to use whether applied by a makeup specialist or by an individual consumer.

As more of the population stay active longer after they reach the golden years of maturity this service is becoming popular in full-service salons.

The authors of *Mature Elegance* offer this service which once belonged only to celebrities, as an additional way to serve your mature clients and increase income in your salon.

Description:

- The Lift consists of two or more very narrow elastic bands having small eyelet rings, or holes, spaced an inch apart for the purpose of adjustment.

- At both ends of an elastic band there are small stem hooks that attach to adhesive tape, covered by a protective paper backing, and having a small hole at one end.

- Lifts are applied before the face is made up. The area where the tapes are to be placed must be dry and free of oil. These areas may be cleansed with rubbing alcohol or astringent.

- Prepare the Lift by placing the stem hook that is on the end of the elastic through the hole in the tape. Do not remove the paper backing until you are ready to apply it to the skin.

Central Florida makeup technician Leslie Ann illustrates, step-by-step, the effectiveness of the Lift.

Fig. 5-10A After

Fig. 5-10 Before: There are few mature women whose appearance cannot be improved by removing (albeit temporarily) obvious sags and deep wrinkles.

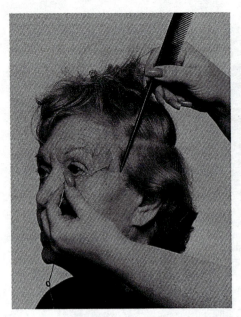

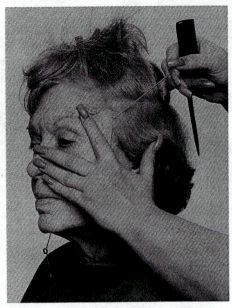

Fig. 5-11 Remove the protective backing from the tape. Place the adhesive side near the outer corner of the eye.

Fig. 5-12 Press on firmly and rub gently for 10 to 15 seconds to assure good contact.

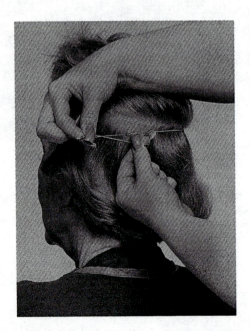

Fig. 5-13 Separate the hair in the back and comb the front part forward. Place adhesive on the opposite side the same distance from the corner of the eye. Pull the elastic band across the head. Place the stem hook in the appropriate eyelet. The skin should not be so taut as to cause the eyes to appear elongated.

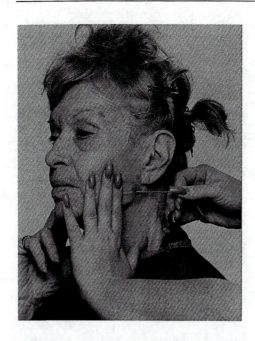

Fig. 5-14 Remove the protective backing from another adhesive tab and position it below the earlobes and near the jawbone. Follow the same instructions for attaching it firmly.

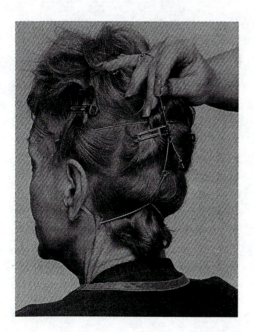

Fig. 5-15 Attach an adhesive in the same position on the opposite side. Pull the elastic band across the head and secure with a bobby pin in the center. Excess length may be cut off or left intact and hidden with a hairpin.

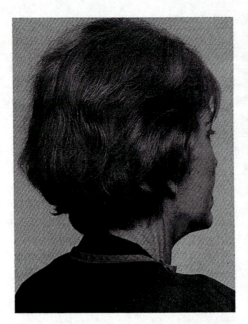

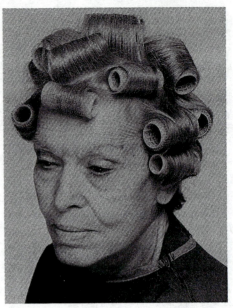

Fig. 5-16 Comb all the hair back over the head to be sure that the bands are well hidden.

Fig. 5-17 Set the hair with Velcro rollers to create volume and mobility. Comb the hair forward and create a style having a fringed face frame to hide any evidence of the adhesive tape.

Fig. 5-18 When the face is made up apply foundation a little heavier over the adhesive tabs and use matte powder to camouflage.

part 2

6

All hairstyles start with a good haircut.

Multiple Services— Featuring "The Haircut" and Color Lightening

Most women depend on regular professional care to keep them looking good.

All hairstyles start with a good haircut. It is the haircut that determines the form, establishes length, and allows for volume or closeness. Most clients, especially those 55 and over, have multiple services including color and perm.

The following step-by-step illustrations are suggested sculpting techniques, often combined with other complementary services.

Each haircut and style is executed on an actual client who was asked to comment on her attitude toward personal appearance as it applies to her. She was asked as well to tell the readers a little of her background and how she, as a person at or over the age of 55, spends her time. It is the opinion of the authors that your mature clients will relate to the philosophies expressed by these ladies and find their comments of interest.

YOUR ROLE AS A BEAUTY CONSULTANT

As women grow older they go through a series of confidence-related stages regarding personal appearance. Many of your aging clients have made personal care a lifelong habit and will continue to do so. In fact, their beauty care professional becomes increasingly important to them. Even the most self-assured women depend on regular professional care to keep them looking good and to bolster their self-esteem. As a rule, mature clients are very dependable and loyal to a salon that has earned their confidence.

Mature clients are inclined to be less adventurous than their younger counterparts. They are less likely to try over-the-counter cosmetics and skin care products. Most readily accept your recommendations pertaining to professional maintenance products, especially those you retail in your salon.

To salute our real-life models and to inspire those who find this book useful, we asked each model to briefly define her philosophy regarding personal appearance and to outline the life experiences that influenced her attitude. In addition, each model's personal analysis, according to our salon professionals, is detailed in a technical chart.

It is a good practice to keep a detailed chart on each of your own clients, listing personal traits as well as products used in the salon and/or sold for home maintenance. It creates a professional bond between you and your client and assists you in future services and product sales.

The ladies selected as models for the *Mature Elegance* text depict an average clientele in an upscale community. While they have varied educational, career, and cultural backgrounds, they have in common a sincere interest in looking their personal best.

The following technical instructions and resulting hairstyles are meant to inspire you to create "elegance" for your own mature clients.

"Whether we like it or not, we are judged immediately by our appearance. I learned early in life that people who look great and have above-average communication skills are the most successful. I felt a competitive urge to excel in whatever role I chose.

"While my professional career has taken many turns, it was always in a 'people-oriented' field. I was a coordinator who planned and produced fashion shows for a prestigious apparel store. I modeled as well, for print ads and in-house fashion reviews. Needless to say all this required a keen sense of personal fashion and self-awareness.

"My hobbies are many and physical fitness tops the list. I am a volunteer political advocate and travel as much as time allows. Four grandchildren keep me busy—and I love every minute of it. I don't believe 'age' is any excuse for letting yourself go. Personal appearance is as important to me today as it ever was."

— Ann

Fig. 6-1 Before

Fig. 6-1A After

ANN: HAIR SHAPING/COLOR LIGHTENING

Hair that has solid-but-uneven patches of gray throughout may be the most challenging to conceal. A technique called color-lightening can be very effective. It is a tedious procedure and must be redone at regular intervals. Still, it is well worth the time and effort as it produces natural high and low lights that emulate nature at its best.

Information pertaining to the condition of Ann's hair and facial features that can be enhanced by makeup and hairstyling is listed. Then the procedure used to arrive at Ann's special look is detailed step-by-step.

MATURE ELEGANCE

Age 55+

Name _Ann_

Ch-6

	Height	Weight	Neck	Shoulders	Face Shape	Eyes	Profile	Hair Analysis	Hair Color
4'9" – 5'									
5'2" – 5'8" +	●								
100–130 lbs.		●							
130–150+ lbs.									
Long									
Short									
Average			●						
Squared									
Rounded				●					
Humped									
Oval									
Square									
Round									
Oval					●				
Convex									
Concave									
Long nose							●		
Upturned nose									
Close									
Wide apart						●			
Normal									
Fine								●	
Coarse									
Sparse									
Dense									
Level 2–4									●
Level 4–5									
Level 5–7									
Level 7–10 (gray)									

Observation:

The hair is 20 percent gray throughout. Eyes are very deep-set and the nose is slightly longer than average. The hair must be softly styled featuring volume on the forehead to balance those facial features.

Fig. 6-2

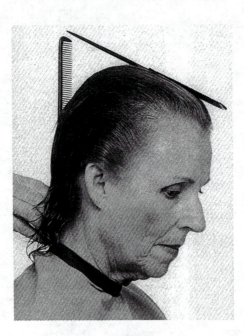

Tint Formula: All-over application (scalp-to-ends)

                    Medium golden blonde—Level 7

Color Lights: High-lift bleach—Level 10 (applied to selected strands)

The Cut:

NOTE:

The base formula results in a warm golden blonde. Color-light formula adds luster and dimension in strategic areas.

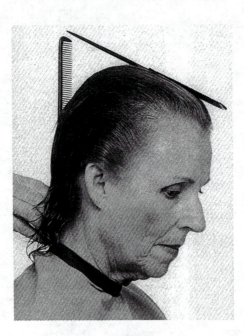

Fig. 6-3 Place a comb flat against the back of the head from the nape to the occipital bone. Position a second comb on the tip of the head. Where the combs pull away from the head determine the "flat and the round" areas. The area between the two indicates the area where volume is needed to balance the head form and facial features.

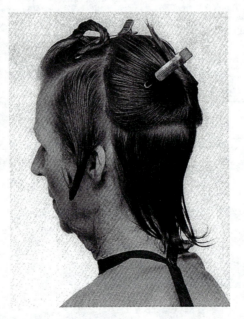

Fig. 6-4 Section the hair from ear to ear at the point where the top comb leaves the head. Divide the back by making a part from ear to ear at the exact point the back comb leaves the head.

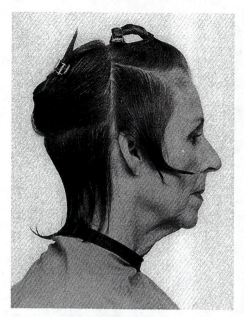

Fig. 6-5   Divide the front forehead area using the corner of each eyebrow as a guide.

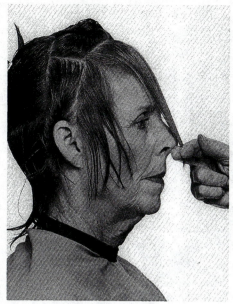

Fig. 6-6   Hold a two-inch panel of hair forward and establish the length using the tip of the nose as a guide.

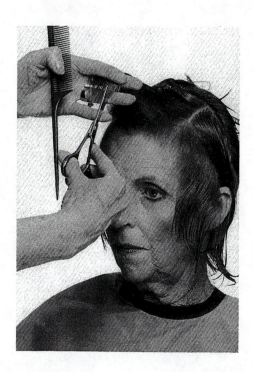

Fig. 6-7   Lift the front guide up at a 45-degree angle and adjust the lengths to coincide from the forehead to the crown.

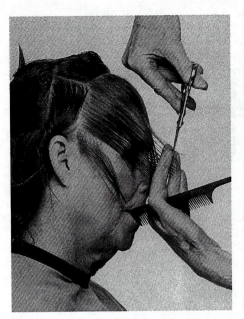

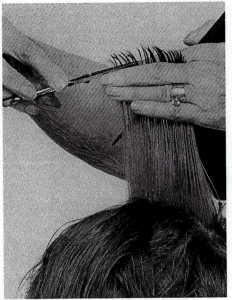

Fig. 6-8   Make a diagonal part one inch into the hairline from the round of the head to the top of the ear. Use the bangs as a guide and cut from the tip of the nose to the front of the ear.

Fig. 6-9   Cut the top section to connect with the crown and front.

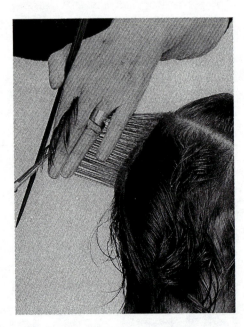

Fig. 6-10   Start in the center crown. Follow the contour of the head and blend with the nape.

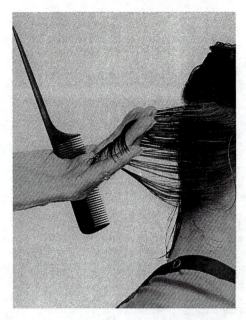

Fig. 6-11 Lift the hair in the nape area away from the head and pull to the center to increase the length on each side. A softly fringed nape is created by lifting the hair up and away from the head form while cutting.

Color Lights

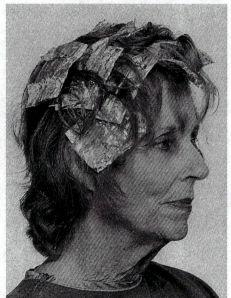

Fig. 6-12 & 13   Weave out selected strands from a panel of hair approximately three inches long and one-half inch wide. Apply high-lift bleach formula and wrap the section in foil pockets. Allow the hair strands to bleach to level 9 or 10. Rinse quickly, taking precautions to keep bleach away from the basic color. A low-volume color enhancer may be applied at this point for a rich color blend.

"In my opinion 'retirement,' as it is literally defined, is overrated. I believe women should be actively involved in an occupation they enjoy as long as possible. That is not to say family and hobbies are not worthwhile occupations. But going to business every day keeps one sharp looking and at the top of their game.

"For eighteen years I was engaged in booking conventions in the fastest-growing international playground in the world. I am now a real estate representative in an upscale country club community. I was top associate the first year I joined the company. I attribute my success to three important factors—skill, attitude, and physical appearance. My ability to produce is judged by potential clients by how well I look.

"I haven't a great deal of time for hobbies inasmuch as I like to spend as much time as possible with my family. However, I am a voracious reader, a gourmet cook, and an avid tennis buff. Nothing deters me from looking my potential best at all times."

—Arra Mae

Fig. 6-14 Before

Fig. 6-14A After

ARRA MAE: GEOMETRIC/BIAS CUT

Some haircuts are so well defined that the necessary support is built into the form. The style is quite durable without the aid of a perm.

A "geometric/bias" cut simply means that all the hair is parted, held, and cut on angles that conform to the natural head form. When the hair falls naturally each section conforms to the one adjacent to it and builds volume and/or closeness to complement the style.

When shaping or sculpting a hair form, the client's facial features and body proportions must be taken into consideration. The chart shown indicates Arra Mae's natural attributes.

MATURE ELEGANCE

Age 55+

Name *Arra Mae*

Ch-6

	Height	Weight	Neck	Shoulders	Face Shape	Eyes	Profile	Hair Analysis	Hair Color
4'9" – 5'									
5'2" – 5'8" +	●								
100–130 lbs.		●							
130–150+ lbs.									
Long			●						
Short									
Average									
Squared				●					
Rounded									
Humped									
Oval					●				
Square									
Round									
Oval									
Convex									
Concave									
Long nose									
Upturned nose							●		
Close						●			
Wide apart									
Normal								●	
Fine									
Coarse									
Sparse									
Dense									
Level 2–4									
Level 4–5									●
Level 5–7									
Level 7–10 (gray)									

Observation:
  Because the shoulders are square and the neck is long, a short hairstyle is very adaptable.

Fig. 6-15

Fig. 6-16 Part the hair in preparation for cutting, from ear to ear arched to a point in the center back just above the occipital bone. At center nape, start cutting angles to the longest point towards the right ear.

Fig. 6-17 From the point cut a straight line toward the earlobe creating an elongated V.

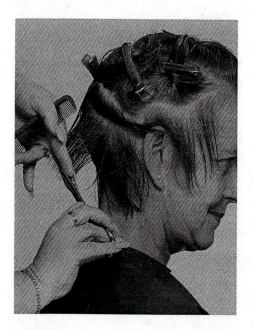

Fig. 6-18 Let down narrow panels of hair from the angled part. Hold the hair down at 45 degrees, using the established nape guide to adjust the length. Repeat the same procedure up the back of the head.

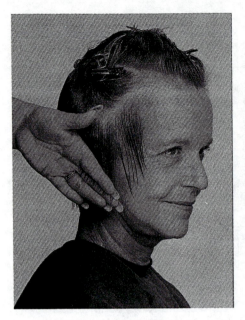 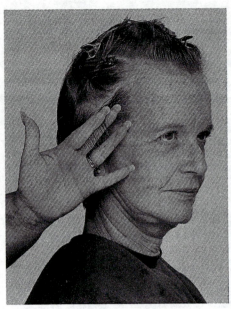

Fig. 6-19 Hold a panel of hair from the previously cut back together with the side section directly over the ear to create a blend. Cut the hair at an angle.

Fig. 6-20 Hold the hair on the side away from the head and at a slight angle. Use the guide established at the blend and cut from the temple toward the earlobe. The perimeter area is softened by the angle.

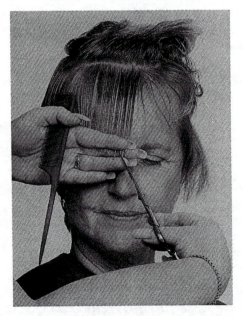

Fig. 6-21 Pull a narrow panel of hair from the forehead area and point-cut to eyebrow length.

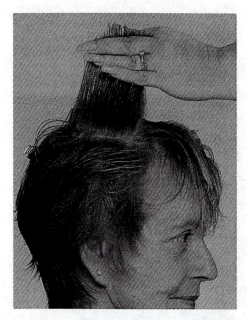

Fig. 6-22 Using the bangs as a guide, hold the hair on the top straight up from the head form and point-cut to the desired length. The hair length is determined by the size of the head. The hair must be left longer on large-size heads.

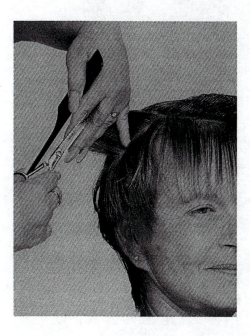

Fig. 6-23 Blend the hair lengths on each side. Balance and blend the lengths in the crown with the perimeter.

NOTE:
....
The hair may be worn straight or curled as adaptable to the client's features.

"I spent many years as an apparel designer. That gave me an appreciation of all facets of fashion. I learned, most of all, while balance, color coordination and design is important, the final result looks best on a figure that is well shaped and a person that is well groomed. For that reason, and of course, self-satisfaction, I am particular about my own appearance.

"After raising three daughters I switched careers. I am now a real estate broker specializing in property management. In retrospect I realize I've always sought positions that allowed me to interact with the public. Personal appearance was always a prerequisite for success.

"I am an artist and have illustrated children's books strictly for relaxation and the desire to diversify my life. I enjoy all types of social activities. Most of all I enjoy taking luxury cruises and short-but-adventurous weekend trips. I believe age is primarily a state of mind. It's how you look and feel that really counts."

—Leona

Fig. 6-24 Before

Fig. 6-24A After

LEONA: MAKEOVER HAIRCUT

Many of my mature clients are long-standing "regulars" and are comfortable wearing a version of the same style, year after year.

Ladies who wear their hair long will usually say they do so because it is easier for them to handle between salon visits. That usually translates into the hair pulled straight away from the face and twisted or held in some way.

The more conservative the client the more reluctant she is to drastically change her hairstyle. However, once the decision is made toward shorter hair, it is almost certain she will go even shorter in the future.

Leona is a typical client who reluctantly agreed to a makeover and was very happy with the results.

The following chart lists pertinent information about the client's hair condition and facial features.

MATURE ELEGANCE

Age 55+

Name *Leona*

Ch-6

	Height	Weight	Neck	Shoulders	Face Shape	Eyes	Profile	Hair Analysis	Hair Color
4'9" – 5'									
5'2" – 5'8" +	●								
100–130 lbs.									
130–150+ lbs.		●							
Long									
Short									
Average			●						
Squared				●					
Rounded									
Humped									
Oval					●				
Square									
Round									
Oval									
Convex									
Concave						●			
Long nose									
Upturned nose							●		
Close									
Wide apart									
Normal									
Fine								●	
Coarse									
Sparse									
Dense									
Level 2–4									
Level 4–5									
Level 5–7									

Observation:

An oval shaped face and up-turned nose is ideal for a hairstyle on or off the face.

Fig. 6-25

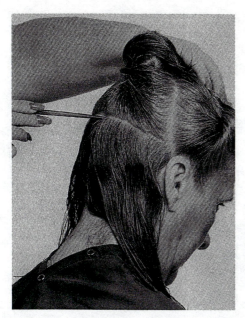

Fig. 6-26 In preparation for the haircut, divide the hair from ear to ear over the crest of the head and make an additional horizontal division from the top of each ear.

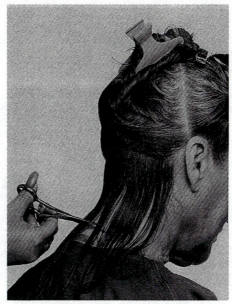

Fig. 6-27 Comb a two-inch panel of hair down and cut a hanging guide at the desired length.

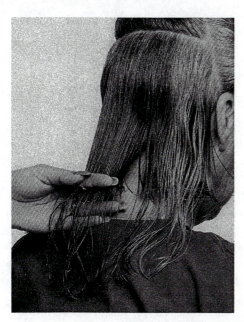

Fig. 6-28 Continue to pull down two-inch panels of hair, lifting slightly away from the head to create minimum elevation until the entire back is completed.

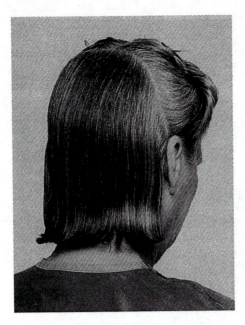

Fig. 6-29 The hair in the back will hang from the crown to the nape at the same length with very little graduation on the ends.

Fig. 6-30 Bring panels of hair down from the side and cut to the same length as the back.

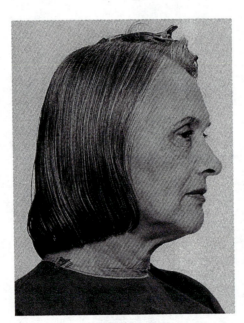

Fig. 6-31 Repeat the same procedure on the opposite side.

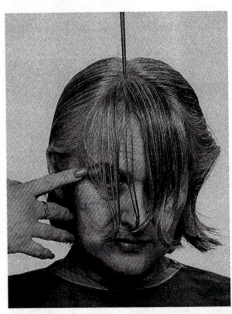

Fig. 6-32 Make a wide triangular section from center crown to the corner of each eyebrow.

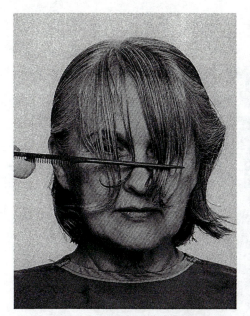

Fig. 6-33 Hold the comb straight across the uncut hair to determine an adaptable length.

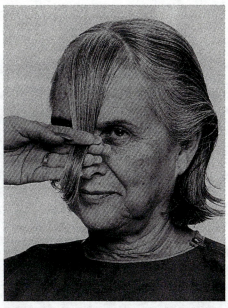

Fig. 6-34 Converge the entire section to the center and cut straight across without elevation.

Fig. 6-35 The completed haircut

Fig. 6-36 Blow-dry the hair and set in hot rollers to provide maximum mobility. The finished hairstyle will have movement but no full circle curls. Use large rollers for best results.

"I can't remember when I was not interested in fashion, but only as it applies to me. I developed my personal style early in life and have always dressed to please myself—never to impress anyone else.

"Before I retired I held an important position with the government in the field of health and nutrition. A BS degree in nutrition opened many doors throughout my working years. I am very health conscious but not in a fanatic sense. I believe physical beauty is equal parts of one's inner self, exercise, and nutritional habits over a long period of time.

"I never think of myself as a 'senior citizen.' That phrase, in my opinion, is anything but inspirational. I've had two good marriages, raised two children and have five grand and four great-grandchildren. In addition, I am a perpetual student. At present I am studying world history and my passionate hobby is playing duplicate (tournament) bridge. I have close friends of all ages and simply have no time to dwell on my own."

—Lydia

Fig. 6-37 Before

Fig. 6-37A After

LYDIA: CLASSIC GRADUATED BOB

A beautiful, durable hairstyle depends almost entirely on the way the hair is shaped. The hair must be cut in a way that allows each and every hair to fall gracefully into place at all times.

Women of all ages lead active lives that most often include on-the-go community activities and health-oriented hobbies such as tennis or golf. To look their best in every role the haircut is the key element.

Pertinent information regarding the condition of the client's hair and her facial features are reviewed. Ways the features may be enhanced by corrective makeup techniques are also suggested. Listed is the step-by-step haircutting procedure used to cut Lydia's beautiful bob.

MATURE ELEGANCE

Age 55+

Name **_Lydia_**

Ch-6

	Height	Weight	Neck	Shoulders	Face Shape	Eyes	Profile	Hair Analysis	Hair Color
4'9" – 5'									
5'2" – 5'8" +	●								
100–130 lbs.									
130–150+ lbs.		●							
Long									
Short			●						
Average			●						
Squared				●					
Rounded									
Humped									
Oval					●				
Square									
Round									
Flat							●		
Convex									
Concave									
Long nose							●		
Upturned nose									
Close									
Wide apart									
Normal									
Fine								●	
Coarse									
Sparse									
Dense								●	
Level 2–4									
Level 4–5									
Level 5–7									
Level 7–10 (gray)									●

Observation:

The hair color is naturally charcoal gray. The nose is quite short and upturned. Most hairstyles are adaptable to these facial features.

Fig. 6-38

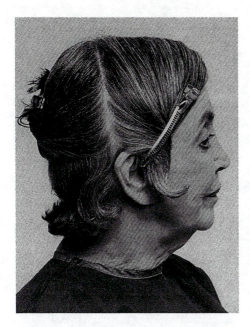

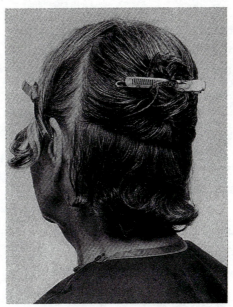

Fig. 6-39 Divide the hair in preparation for an asymmetric bob. Part the hair on the side using the center eyebrow as a guide, to indicate a heavy overlay on one side.

Fig. 6-40 Make a part from ear to ear over the crest of the head and a horizontal part from ear to ear just under the occipital bone. That area is considered the flat of the head and determines the extent of graduation before creating a solid weight line.

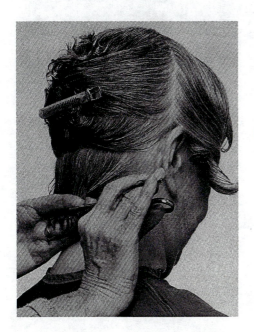

Fig. 6-41 Start the haircut at center nape. Hold the hair straight down with tension. Pull all the hair toward center nape and slightly away from the nape. Cut straight across to establish a soft zero length at the center that gradually increases in length toward each ear.

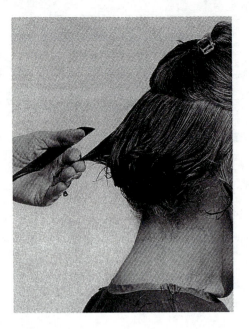

Fig. 6-42 Bring down narrow panels of hair from horizontal partings. Picking up the previously cut section as a guide, lift the hair about 45 degrees away from the head and cut. Follow this procedure until all of the lower section has been cut. A slight graduation is created by the way the hair is held while cutting.

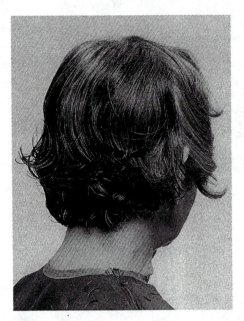

Fig. 6-43 Bring all the hair down in the back and cut to the longest length established in the lower section. This procedure creates a soft weight line.

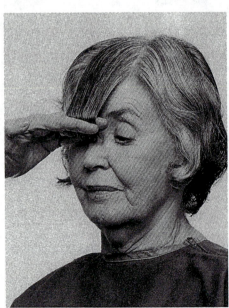

Fig. 6-44 Make a triangular section from eyebrow to eyebrow. Hold the panel of hair forward and cut to the bridge of the nose.

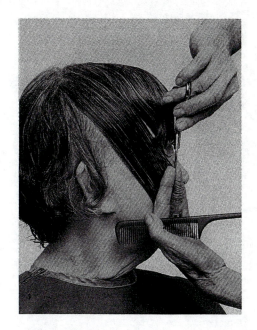

Fig. 6-45 Comb all the hair on the heavy side forward and down at an angle following the jawline. Using the bangs as a guide, cut the face frame at an angle from that point to the chin.

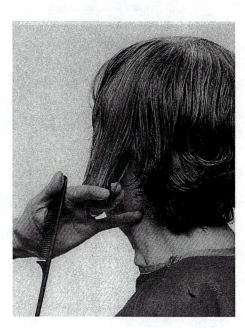

Fig. 6-46 Hold down the hair on the opposite side and establish a hanging length to coincide with the back guide.

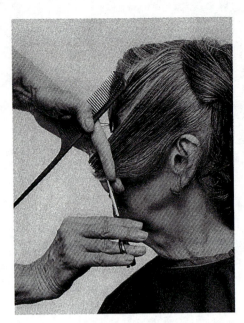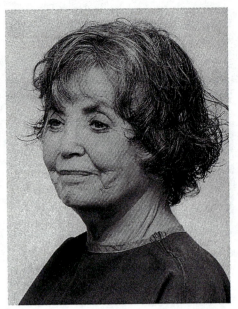

Fig. 6-47 Using the hanging length as a guide, pull the hair forward at an angle from partings following the contour of the head. Cut a face frame using the same procedure as the opposite side.

Fig. 6-48 When the perimeter lengths have been established, hold the hair away from the head and check for uneven lengths throughout. Take care not to shorten the hair (only remove irregular ends). Shorter lengths throughout would create unwanted layering.

"It's not less important to me to look good at this age than it was when I was much younger. It was never important to me to be a 'trend setter,' nor did I feel compelled to be a trend follower. My college years were filled with activity and I never let marriage and a family slow me down.

"My husband was a pilot and we met and married during the war. I felt fulfilled just to be his wife and helpmate. We raised two beautiful children and now have three grandchildren.

"I am a member of The Chi Omega Alumni Sorority, American Philatelic Society, and [am] an aggressive stamp collector. To add color to my life I collect antique postcards of the Victorian era and nineteenth-century valentines. I also collect turn-of-the-century illustrator art and have contributed to a number of books on this subject. I sure don't dwell on the very natural process of aging—I simply try to make every day count for something good."

—June

Jane

Fig. 6-49 Before

Fig. 6-49A After

JANE: HAIRCUT/STYLE/TEMPORARY RINSE

The most important factor in servicing mature clients, as with all clients, is to satisfy the individual. In order to do that the person must be pleased with the image she sees once the style is complete.

It is also important to realize that a person seldom sees herself as others see her. She has a personal view of her physical appearance and often feels uncomfortable and self-conscious wearing a hairstyle that she feels is unflattering.

The more conservative the individual, the less apt she is to drastically change the color of her hair as she grows older. She is far more comfortable having a simple temporary rinse that enhances the natural gray color and gives the hair a lively shine.

A hairstyle should be balanced to frame the size and shape of the face. The same principles apply to adaptable face framing that apply to selecting an appropriate frame for a beautiful painting. It must feature the face in a flattering way. If the facial features are large, the hair must have enough volume to balance the entire head form.

As part of a permanent record file kept for each client, Jane's facial features and body proportions were taken into consideration when creating an adaptable hairstyle.

MATURE ELEGANCE

Age 55+

Name **_Jane_**

Ch-6

	Height	Weight	Neck	Shoulders	Face Shape	Eyes	Profile	Hair Analysis	Hair Color
4'9" – 5'									
5'2" – 5'8" +	•								
100–130 lbs.									
130–150+ lbs.		•							
Long									
Short			•						
Wide									
Squared									
Rounded				•					
Humped									
Oval									
Square									
Round					•				
Flat									
Convex						•			
Concave									
Long nose									
Upturned nose							•		
Close									
Wide apart									
Normal									
Fine									
Coarse								•	
Sparse									
Dense								•	
Level 2–4									
Level 4–5									
Level 5–7									
Level 7–10 (gray)									•

Observation:

100 percent gray/platinum rinse

Fig. 6-50

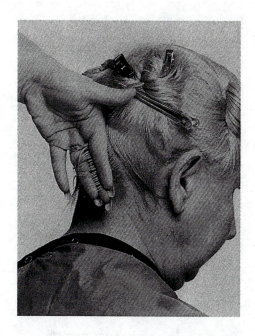

Fig. 6-51 First shampoo the hair and apply a temporary rinse to add shine and remove any yellow tinges. Then divide the hair into easy-to-handle sections. Start at the nape area and remove bulk and length to create a softly fitted look.

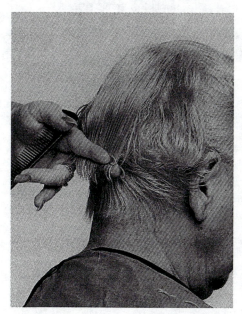

Fig. 6-52 Increase the length from zero to approximately two inches at an area that coincides with the middle of the ear.

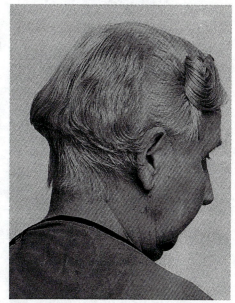

Fig. 6-53 Continue cutting up the back of the head. Let down narrow panels of hair cut to the length at mid-ear. This creates a definite weight line.

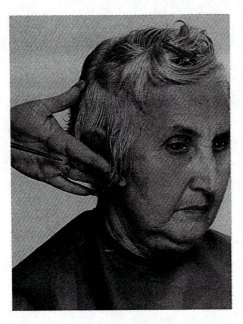

Fig. 6-54 Make a horizontal part at the temple and cut the hair to blend with the weight line in the back.

Fig. 6-55 Bring narrow horizontal panels down from the side and cut to the initial guide until the entire side is complete. Repeat the same cutting procedure on the opposite side.

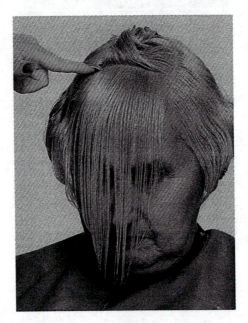

Fig. 6-56 Make a part approximately two inches behind the hairline and comb the hair forward.

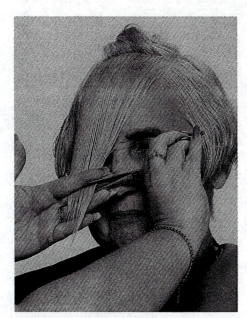 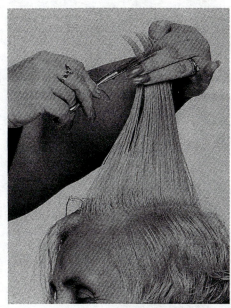

Fig. 6-57 Holding the hair at a 45-degree angle from the forehead, cut the hair to the same length as the sides.

Fig. 6-58 Using the established lengths on each side, back, and front, blend the lengths throughout.

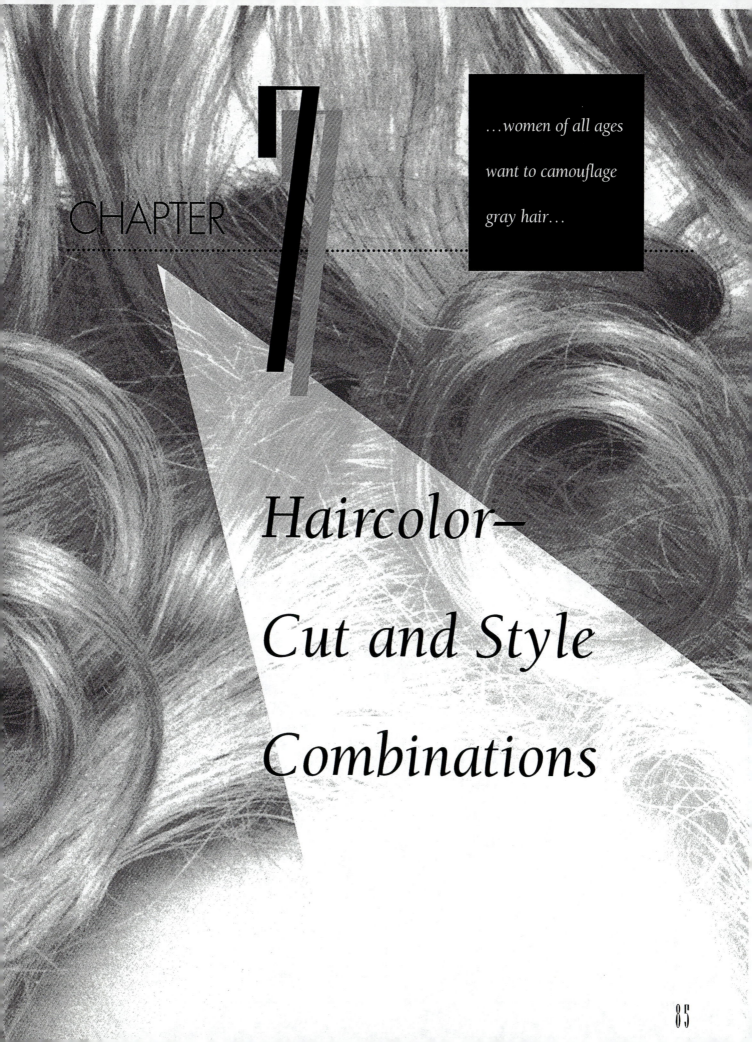

7

*…women of all ages
want to camouflage
gray hair…*

Haircolor–

Cut and Style

Combinations

For no known reason, an increasing number of people living in the last half of the twentieth century turn gray at an earlier age than did their ancestors. According to manufacturers of haircolor products, this information is significant not only to the sale of their product, but to salon professionals who render haircolor services to their clients.

We know the reason, however, that women of all ages want to camouflage gray hair, which inevitably indicates "old age." Women are a greater part of the American workforce than ever in history, and a greater number are choosing to work longer. Many are forced to compete with younger people in the job market and are anxious to look as young as possible.

This chapter focuses on haircolor but is not limited to any one service. A combination of services is required to keep clients looking their personal best.

The ladies in this chapter speak for themselves as to the importance of looking good.

"I simply do not believe in retiring if it means bringing an active business life to a sudden halt. For that reason I am as active now as I was when I was a successful real estate broker. I choose, however, to diversify my activities to make more time for my husband and family.

"I work part-time as a representative of the Orlando Orange County Convention and Visitors Bureau (OCCVB). My position requires me to negotiate with high-profile business executives. I must have the appearance at all times of a capable business person. My physical appearance has a lot to do with how successful I am.

"In addition to my extended business career I am very busy doing volunteer work for the Council for Aging (Seniors First). Duplicate bridge is my favorite hobby, but by no means my only one. I am an avid golfer and I travel with my husband here and abroad, for business and pleasure. I also walk three to four miles each day. Need I tell you that I firmly believe health and beauty go hand in hand? I have no intention of neglecting either."

—Helen

Helen

Fig. 7-1 Before

Fig. 7-1A After

HELEN: DIMENSIONAL BLONDE TOUCH-UP

Many graying adults opt for a totally blonde look. In order to avoid such an artificial look use a formula that has a lively, natural appearance even though it decolorizes to level 10.

Two complementary shades of tint will produce a dimensional illusion in the hair that looks very natural. The natural color of most people's hair is indeed dimensional, meaning only that it has more than one level of color throughout. Blondes most often are much lighter in the front than in the back and nape area. By applying color to graying hair to replicate that natural effect, the object is to enhance the client's appearance without an obvious artificial look.

Helen's original hair color and the formula used is listed below. Listed as well, in her chart, are details of facial features that can be enhanced by an adaptable hairstyle and corrective makeup.

MATURE ELEGANCE
Age 55+
Name ___*Helen*___
Ch- 7

	Height	Weight	Neck	Shoulders	Face Shape	Eyes	Profile	Hair Analysis	Hair Color
4'9" – 5'									
5'2" – 5'8" +	●								
100–130 lbs.									
130–150+ lbs.		●							
Long			●						
Short									
Average									
Squared				●					
Rounded									
Humped									
Oval					●				
Square									
Round									
Oval									
Convex									
Concave							●		
Long nose									
Upturned nose									
Close									
Wide apart						●			
Normal									
Fine									
Coarse								●	
Sparse									
Dense									
Level 2–4									
Level 4–5									
Level 5–7									
Level 7–10 (gray)									●

Observation:
Hair is 30 percent gray throughout. She has a receding chin.

Fig. 7-2

Bleach Formulas

1. Light (high-lift) blonde tint (level 10)
   Equal amount of 30-volume peroxide

2. Blonde beige tint (level 7)
   Equal amount of 20-volume peroxide

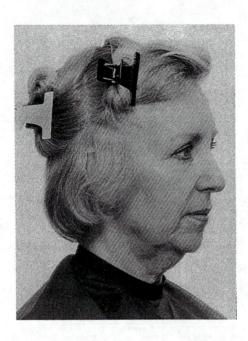

Fig. 7-3 Divide the top area from the lower section by parting the hair starting at the temple and following the natural curve of the head.

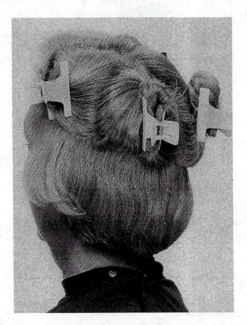

Fig. 7-4 Extend the divisions from each temple to the center back ending just below the occipital bone.

Fig. 7-5   Mix both formulas, each in a separate bowl, before starting the color procedure.

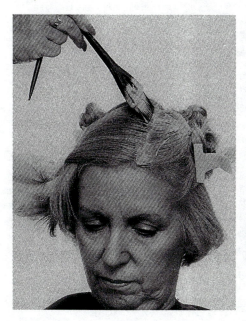

Fig. 7-6   Start applying the color (formula 1) in the center front. Make narrow horizontal partings and apply to the new growth.

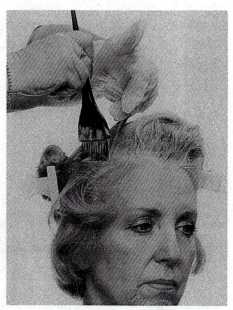

Fig. 7-7   Continue the application from center part to the entire side.

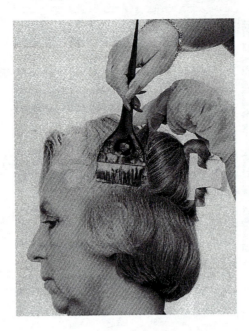

Fig. 7-8 Repeat the same application procedure on the opposite side.

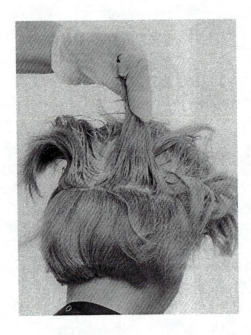

Fig. 7-9 When high-lift formula has been applied to both sides and the front, start at center crown and carefully apply the same formula to the entire back down to the occipital bone.

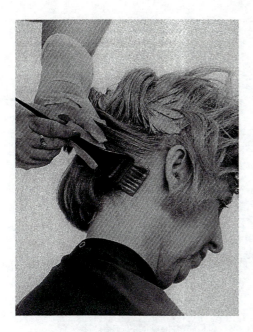

Fig. 7-10 Apply the darkest tint (formula 2) to the lower back and nape area. When all the new growth has been covered, allow it to process 20 minutes.

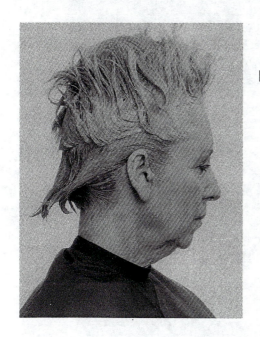

Fig. 7-11 When the new growth has sufficiently processed, pull the color through to the ends and process an additional ten minutes. Rinse thoroughly and lightly shampoo the hair with a color-safe cleansing product. Finish with a conditioning rinse. The hair at this point is ready to be styled.

"My productive life started in New York City, where I held a variety of administrative and financial management positions. My business administration training at Hunter College opened a number of doors, but I was attracted, early on, to the excitement and pace of the advertising and public relations industry. I soon learned that, in an 'image' business, personal appearance is an important element in the professionalism required for success.

"I stayed in the advertising/PR field—eventually becoming managing partner of a Florida ad agency—until my recent retirement.

"I now spend my time traveling, surf fishing at our beach condo, and trying to improve my tennis game. I'm also sharpening the gourmet cooking skills that got a little rusty during my professional years.

"Although business is no longer a part of my life, my personal appearance is just as important as ever. Growing older can be pleasant if one's attitude is right, and caring for my appearance is vital to my attitude."

— Regina

Regina

Fig. 7-12 Before

Fig. 7-12A After

REGINA: COLOR CONTRASTING

Most women whose hair is turning gray want to disguise it or make this natural progression of life a little less prominent. They want just as much for the "cover-up" to be a subject that stays in the salon.

Skilled salon technicians devise various ways to make all haircolor look as if it is the work of nature. A technique called "contrasting" is very effective.

The use of a cap to change the color of selected hair strands is not a new technique. The selection of contrasting formulas makes the difference.

The formula for Regina's hair color and her facial features are analyzed in the following chart.

MATURE ELEGANCE

Age 55+

Name ___*Regina*___

Ch-7

	Height	Weight	Neck	Shoulders	Face Shape	Eyes	Profile	Hair Analysis	Hair Color
4'9" – 5'									
5'2" – 5'8" +	●								
100–130 lbs.									
130–150+ lbs.		●							
Long			●						
Short									
Average									
Squared				●					
Rounded									
Humped									
Oval					●				
Square									
Round									
Flat							●		
Convex									
Concave									
Long nose									
Upturned nose									
Close									
Wide apart									
Normal						●			
Fine								●	
Coarse									
Sparse									
Dense								●	
Level 2–4									
Level 4–5									
Level 5–7									●
Level 7–10 (gray)									

Observation:

The eyes are small with heavy lids. The hair is fine but plentiful. The hair is frosted to create softness to complement facial features.

Fig. 7-13

The Contrast Application

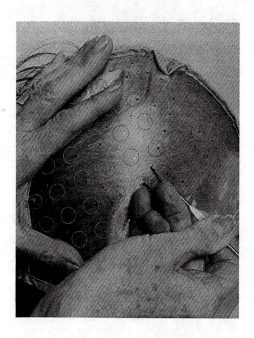

Fig. 7-14 Comb all the hair straight away from the face and cover with a plastic frosting cap. Tie the cap under the chin so it will not move during the procedure. Pull narrow strands of hair through the holes indicated for the amount of hair you wish to contrast. Work up both sides and back and front.

Fig. 7-15 Pull the hair partway through to make a small loop. Short hair is inclined to pull all the way through, but as nearly as possible make small loops as shown.

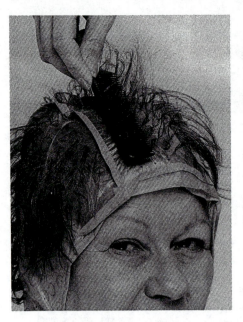

Fig. 7-16 Use a comb to pull the hair all the way through the holes in the cap.

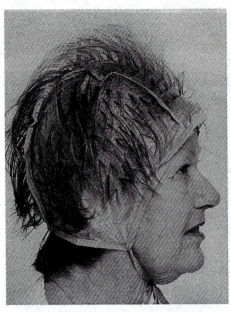

Fig. 7-17 Be sure all the hair is pulled straight out from the selected hole. (Most caps have alternate holes that can be used if more contrast is desired.)

NOTE:
....

When the desired amount of color has been lifted from the hair, rinse the bleach from outside of the cap; remove the cap and lightly shampoo the hair. The hair is now ready to be shaped.

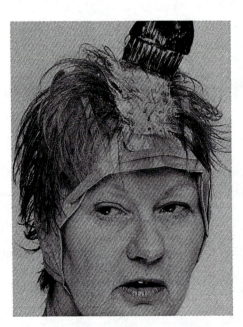

Fig. 7-18 Mix high-lift tint or bleach and carefully apply to all exposed strands using a tint brush.

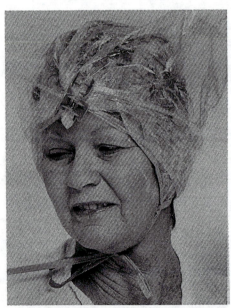

Fig. 7-19 Cover the frosting cap with a plastic bag and process for 15 to 20 minutes.

The Hair Cut

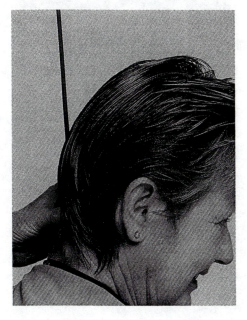

Fig. 7-20 Hold a comb flat against the head at the lower nape. Where the head curves away from the comb is the proper place to divide the hair horizontally from ear to ear in preparation for the shaping.

Fig. 7-21 From narrow vertical partings, hold the hair in the nape area 45 degrees from the head and cut. This holding position creates a softly fringed nape.

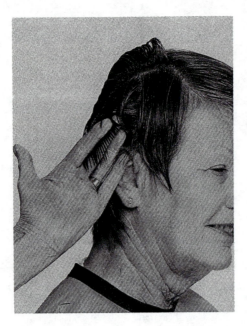

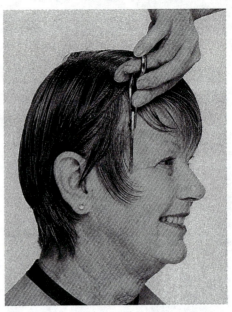

Fig. 7-22 Continue to let narrow panels of hair down as you work up the head in the back and behind each ear.

Fig. 7-23 Cut the hair on the side on an angle from temple to the sideburn area.

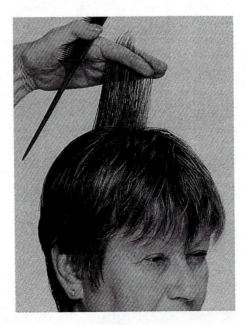

Fig. 7-24 When the perimeter shaping is complete, cut the top and forefront to blend with the sides and back lengths.

"I subscribe to the belief that one's personal appearance sets the tone for perceived competence. I have spent most of my career prominently entrenched in the world of finance. When interviewing clients who are contemplating large financial investments, personal trust is of utmost importance. Right or wrong, if you look professional you are considered to be trustworthy.

"I am a branch manager for the third largest bank, nationwide—Home Savings of America— and I supervise a young energetic staff. They are required to present a professional appearance at all times. And I realize I must be their role model.

"Even when relaxing in my garden I still feel the necessity to look my casual best. In my opinion, if you look good, you feel good about yourself— and that's important to me."

— Taffy

Taffy

Fig. 7-25 Before

Fig. 7-25A After

TAFFY: ALLOVER TINT TOUCH-UP

The hair of most people over 55 has varying percentages of gray. Not everyone wants to cover it completely but most want to camouflage its prominence.

There are a variety of reasons why women want to disguise the fact they are growing gray. Often it is because they are still involved in a career that requires them to compete with much younger contenders for their job.

In order to cover gray completely—to keep, as nearly as possible, the natural hair color—a tint formula must be applied from the scalp to the ends. Hair grows approximately one-half inch every four weeks and, depending on the percentage of gray, the new growth will become obvious.

An allover tint process requires a firm commitment from the client and a professional responsibility from the salon technician.

Listed is pertinent information regarding the condition of the client's hair and facial features insofar as can be corrected (or improved) by standard salon services. Following are step-by-step instructions to Taffy's professional look.

NOTE:

1 part 7 Natural
1 part Red Violet
Equal clear 20 vol peroxide

This formula will lift natural color medium dark brown four to five shades and completely cover the 20 percent gray that is concentrated in the front.

MATURE ELEGANCE Age 55+ Name __Taffy__ Ch-7	Height	Weight	Neck	Shoulders	Face Shape	Eyes	Profile	Hair Analysis	Hair Color
4'9" – 5'									
5'2" – 5'8" +	●								
100–130 lbs.									
130–150+ lbs.		●							
Long			●						
Short									
Wide			●						
Squared									
Rounded				●					
Humped									
Oval					●				
Square									
Round									
Flat									
Convex									
Concave									
Long nose									
Upturned nose									
Close									
Wide apart						●			
Normal							●		
Fine (Med.)								●	
Coarse									
Sparse									
Dense									
Level 2–4									
Level 4–5									●
Level 5–7									
Level 7–10 (gray)									

Observation:
Prominent chin — sparse eyebrows.

Fig. 7-26

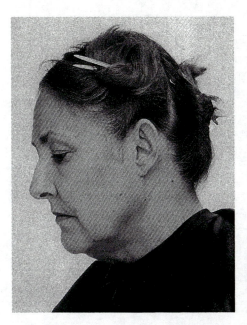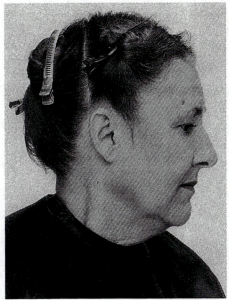

Fig. 7-27 & 28   Divide the hair into four, easy-to-handle sections by parting the hair in the center from forehead to nape and from ear to ear over the crest of the head.

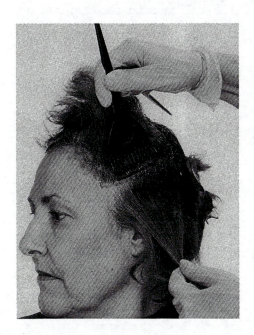

Fig. 7-29 Start applying tint formula to the outgrowth at the scalp. The width of the partings depends entirely on the density of the hair. If the hair is thick, make narrow, horizontal partings and be sure the tint thoroughly saturates each section from the scalp down the strand sufficient to cover the new growth. Work from the ear to center forehead.

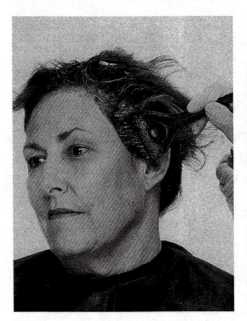

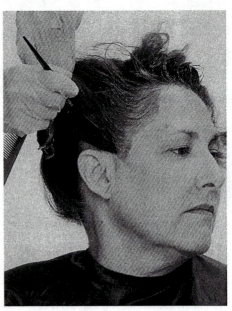

Fig. 7-30 Apply tint to the hairline. Be sure every strand is completely saturated.

Fig. 7-31 Repeat the same procedure on the opposite side. Carefully apply tint to the entire hairline and check to see the hairline is well saturated as this is the first area that begins to fade.

Fig. 7-32 Start at the top of one of the back sections. Make partings that follow the natural contour of the head and apply tint generously to the new growth. Apply tint to the entire back down to the occipital bone.

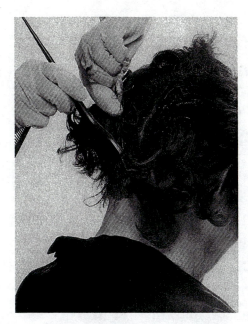

Fig. 7-33 When the occipital area is reached start applying tint from the nape up to the previous application.

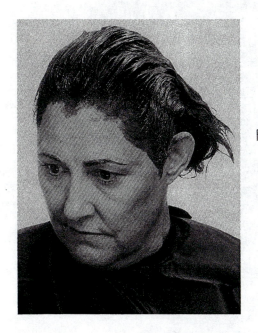

Fig. 7-34 Using a wide-tooth tint comb, immediately pull the tint through to the ends. With gloved hands separate the hair strands. Allow the tint to process for 30–40 minutes or until the desired color has been reached.

NOTE:

When the tint has sufficiently processed, rinse thoroughly and shampoo the hair using a color-safe cleansing product. The hair at this point is ready to style.

"It has been said the luckiest people are those that make a living doing what they love most. That makes me extremely fortunate indeed. I am a personal shopper. I can't remember when I didn't enjoy shopping for myself. It is double the fun to shop for others! While shopping is an avocation it gives me a tremendous advantage toward current fashion as a whole and my own tastes in particular.

"I am still actively engaged in a day-to-day business world. I work for a prominent interior design firm. It's surprising how it relates to the art of design and fashion.

"My hobbies are so diversified I find it difficult to articulate my favorite one. If I must, I would say bird watching and photography top the list. I was born and raised in a wonderful vacation land and one needn't look for hobbies in an environment so rich in activities. Three daughters and three grandchildren help keep me feeling young—I keep myself looking young."

— Betty Jo

Betty Jo

Fig. 7-35 Before

Fig. 7-35A After

BETTY JO: DIMENSIONAL CONTRAST TOUCH-UP

Some mature women rather like the looks of their hair when it starts to turn gray. They object however when the percentage of gray outweighs the natural color. Dimensional contrasting is a great solution.

The object is to tint most of the hair to the client's natural color then bleach selected strands to look as if just a little gray is scattered throughout.

Even Betty Jo's closest friends do not know exactly what, if anything, she does to make her hair look so great. She has a new-growth touch-up (natural color only) every four weeks. Then at every third touch-up, contrast strands are renewed and her hair is reshaped.

Betty Jo's hair condition and facial features were analyzed to illustrate how a hairstyle and makeup can indeed make a world of difference in one's appearance (see her chart).

MATURE ELEGANCE

Age 55+

Name _Betty Jo_

Ch-7

	Height	Weight	Neck	Shoulders	Face Shape	Eyes	Profile	Hair Analysis	Hair Color
4'9" – 5'									
5'2" – 5'8" +	●								
100–130 lbs.									
130–150+ lbs.		●							
Long			●						
Short									
Wide									
Squared				●					
Rounded									
Humped									
Oval					●				
Square									
Round									
Normal						●			
Convex									
Concave									
Long nose									
Upturned nose									
Close									
Wide apart									
Normal							●		
Fine								●	
Coarse									
Sparse									
Dense									
Level 2–4									
Level 4–5									
Level 5–7									
Level 7–10 (gray)									●

Observation:

Small eyes — gray hair in the front only.

Fig. 7-36

Tint formula

1 part light brown (level 6)

1 part natural beige gold

Equal parts 20-volume peroxide

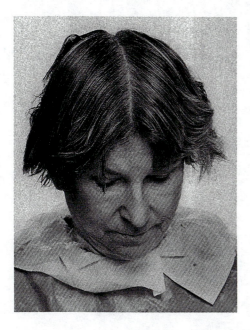

Fig. 7-37 Part the hair from the forehead to the highest part of the crown. Extend the part from the crown to the nape down the center back. Then divide the front and back by making a part from ear to ear over the crest of the head.

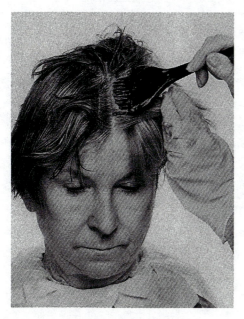

Fig. 7-38 Apply tint formula to the new growth only. Take care not to overlap the tint onto the contrasting strands. Begin the application in the front.

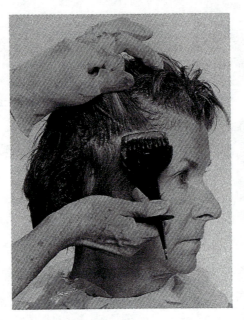

Fig. 7-39 Make narrow partings and apply tint to the new growth on each side from center part to the sideburn area.

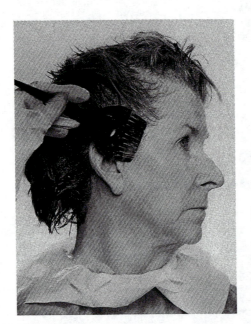

Fig. 7-40 Reapply tint to the entire hairline that frames the face.

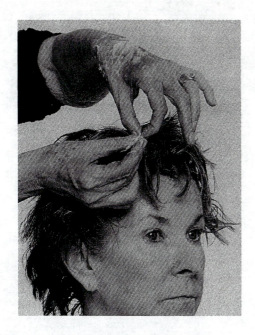

Fig. 7-41 For quick access to the protective cream put a dollop on the back of one hand and go carefully throughout making sure that each light strand is protected.

Fig. 7-42 Apply protective cream to all the contrast strands to keep them free from the tint application. Process according to manufacturer's instructions or until the desired level of color is deposited. The processing period is usually 20 to 30 minutes. First, quickly rinse the tint from the hair using a strong spray, then lightly shampoo the hair using a color-safe cleansing product. The hair is now ready to be styled.

114

CHAPTER

8

Very often the hair
of women 55 and
older begins to soften
and thin.

Focus on Perms–

The Chemical

Foundation of

Hairstyles

Very often the hair of women 55 and older begins to soften and thin. The body that held a hairstyle in place from one salon visit to another seems to dissipate. A perm for the purpose of supporting the haircut becomes more and more important.

Technology related to the chemical service called *perming* has progressed to a point that all types of hair can now be successfully permed to whatever degree of body or curl desired.

The hairstyles in Chapter 8 are all enhanced by a perm but are far from limited to that one service. Most, as you will find when you review the step-by-step information, have haircolor and all have precision hairstyles.

While no lady is willing to tell her age, each of these models is 55 or older. Not that you would guess, but the youngest model is just 55, the oldest is 80. Each tell in their own words how and why they stay looking so great.

"I am an artist—dedicated to expressing myself in a way that makes a statement about who I am and what generates the boundless energy required for this extraordinary mode of communication.

"I don't dwell on my physical appearance as I firmly believe personal image is a reflection of one's innermost dreams and vibrations of the spirit. I depend on a salon professional to keep me looking my potential best.

"I have always equated life with the excitement of a circus—illusion and a carousel whirling through myriad lights. Like the beautiful horses on a carousel, life is filled with ups and downs—a journey that encounters both comedy and pathos. Art is the center of my private universe which allows me the confidence to share my creative energy. I give myself permission to be different and present the theater of the absurd, or to be as outrageous as I want to be. Fanciful childhood images locked in my memory are a source of unexplainable euphoria and an endless inspiration for my creative efforts."

—Phyllis

Phyllis

Fig. 8-1 Before

Fig. 8-1A After

PHYLLIS: DIAGONAL PERM WRAP

The stability of a professional salon depends on regular (repeat) clients—those who return every four to six weeks for services.

Phyllis wears her hair very short supported by a perm in the crown area. The hair normally grows one-half inch a month. This client wants to keep her hair at the same length all the time, so she requires a shaping about every six weeks and a perm about every three to four months.

The length a mature person should wear her hair is determined by her body proportions. Short hair looks great on petite women. Phyllis is only five foot three and has a youthful body frame. She is perfect for a short, short hairstyle.

The haircut is detailed step-by-step and the fully wrapped perm is shown for direction.

MATURE ELEGANCE
Age 55+
Name _Phyllis_
Ch. 8

	Height	Weight	Neck	Shoulders	Face Shape	Eyes	Profile	Hair Analysis	Hair Color
4'9" – 5'									
5'2" – 5'8" +	●								
100–130 lbs.									
130–150+ lbs.		●							
Long									
Short			●						
Average									
Squared									
Rounded				●					
Humped									
Oval									
Square									
Round									
Pear					●				
Convex							●		
Concave									
Long nose									
Upturned nose									
Close						●			
Wide apart									
Normal									
Fine								●	
Coarse									
Sparse								●	
Dense									
Level 2–4									
Level 4–5									
Level 5–7									
Level 7–10 (gray)									●

Observation:
Very adaptable features

Fig. 8-2

The Perm

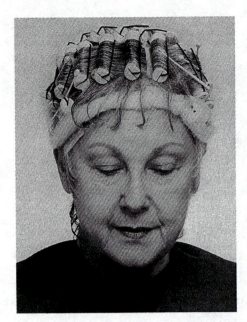

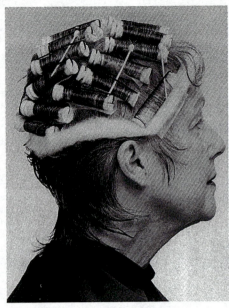

Fig. 8-3 Medium-size perm rods are positioned on base from an off-center part from temple to temple. Perm rods are directed away from the part on each side.

Fig. 8-4 The hair is wrapped to follow the natural contour of the head, resulting in a diagonal positioning ending behind the ear.

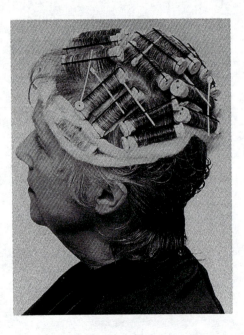

Fig. 8-5 The same wrapping procedure is followed on the opposite side.

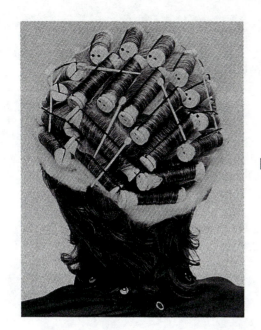

Fig. 8-6 Position medium-size perm rods at an angle from the off-center part to the occipital bone. Fill in each back panel by placing horizontal perm rods behind each ear and at the center back.

The Cut

Fig. 8-7 Make a divisional part separating the crown area from the perimeter (the flat of the head).

Fig. 8-8 Start shaping behind the ear by combing all the hair up from the nape to the divisional part and cutting the hair to a length of approximately one and one-half inches.

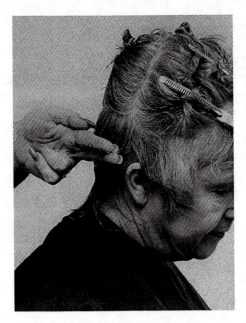

Fig. 8-9   Let down a panel of hair and cut to the guideline.

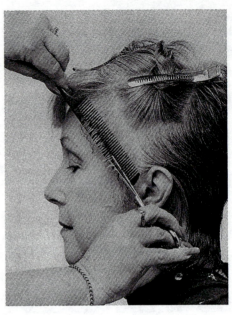

Fig. 8-10   Bring the hair forward; lift slightly away from the face and cut to a length of one inch. Lifting the hair away from the face creates a softened, fringy face frame.

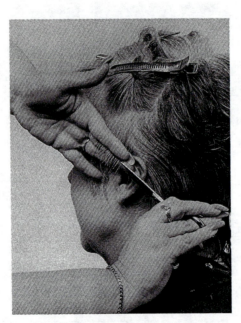

Fig. 8-11   Bring diagonal panels of hair down to the guide, lift slightly away from the head and cut so the length increases toward the crown. Continue this procedure to center crown.

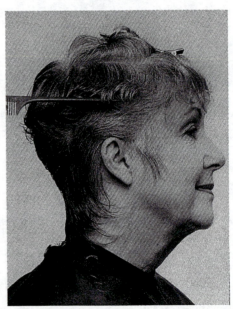

Fig. 8-12   Horizontally check and blend the lengths on each side.

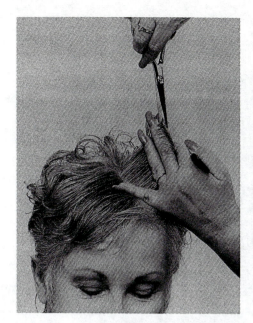

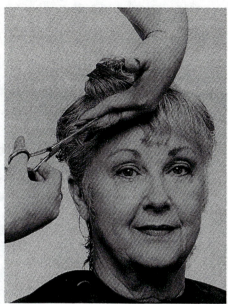

Fig. 8-13 Hold the hair throughout the front and crown straight up from its base and cut the lengths to approximately three inches.

Fig. 8-14 Comb narrow strands of hair onto the forehead and point-cut to create a light fringe.

"I've lived in sunny Florida since 1983, where lifestyles are more casual than they were in Milwaukee, Wisconsin, where I grew up. However, I never succumbed to the habit of some of Florida's natives who practically live in shorts and T-shirts the year 'round. I think I owe it to myself to look my very best at all times.

"Acrylic painting and soft sculpture are my artistic outlets. I paint for my own pleasure and my friends compliment my talent by requesting pieces of my original work. Soft sculpture is extremely satisfying inasmuch as it requires imagination and unique skill. I recently was engaged by a prominent Italian restaurateur to create soft sculpture for the walls of his beautiful establishment.

"I am deeply involved in volunteer work for the Florida Conservation Association; the purpose is to preserve the natural beauty of the state. For exercise and sheer pleasure I play tennis when the weather permits."

—Lois

Lois

Fig. 8-15 Before

Fig. 8-15A After

LOIS: HALO PERM/SEMI-PERMANENT COLOR

Just because a client is classified by age as "mature" does not necessarily mean she is less active than some of her younger counterparts.

Some clients have neither the time nor patience to sit for hours in a beauty salon. Those ladies will be loyal regulars if you can design a grooming resume that requires very little time in the salon and is easily maintained.

An ideal combination of services for a busy client is a short, well-balanced haircut, a standard allover perm, and a semi-permanent haircolor that last from four to six weeks and fades off without revealing any obvious outgrowth.

The time Lois spends for all her beauty services is less than two hours. She has a perm every three months and a haircolor with each perm and once in between. It is perfect timing for her lifestyle.

The hairstyle designed for Lois is by no means for convenience only. It takes into consideration her facial features and body proportions. A permanent record is kept on file and updated regularly.

MATURE ELEGANCE
Age 55+
Name ___Lois___
Ch- 8

	Height	Weight	Neck	Shoulders	Face Shape	Eyes	Profile	Hair Analysis	Hair Color
4'9" – 5'									
5'2" – 5'8" +	●								
100–130 lbs.									
130–150+ lbs.		●							
Long			●						
Short									
Average									
Squared				●					
Rounded									
Humped									
Oval					●				
Square									
Round									
Pear									
Convex									
Concave							●		
Long nose									
Upturned nose									
Close									
Wide apart									
Normal						●			
Fine								●	
Coarse									
Sparse									
Dense									
Level 2–4									
Level 4–5									
Level 5–7									
Level 7–10 (gray)									●

Observation:
Facial features best suited to short hairstyles.

Fig. 8-16

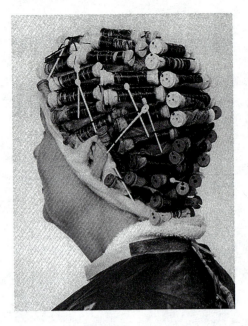

Fig. 8-17 Section the hair into panels no wider than the length of the perm rod being used. Select a rod having a diameter that allows the hair to go around a minimum of one and one-half revolutions. Subsection each panel the width of each perm rod.

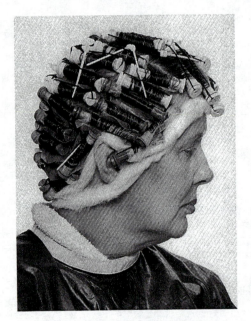

Fig. 8-18 Working from the crown toward the nape, position on-base rods in narrow horizontal subsections until all areas of the head are wrapped.

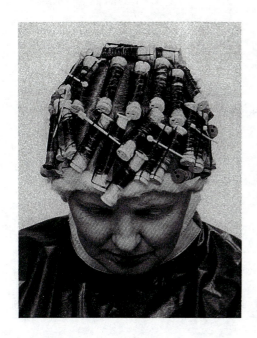

Fig. 8-19 Direct the hair in the forefront on zigzag bases so it has no definite direction but can be worn casually tousled.

Fig. 8-20 When the perm wrap is complete, place a protective strip of cotton around the face frame, over the ears, and across the nape. Follow manufacturer's instructions and process the perm to a firm, springy curl formation followed by appropriate neutralization.

Fig. 8-21 After the perm is complete, towel the hair to a damp stage and apply semi-permanent haircolor at the shampoo bowl. Because the color formula contains no ammonia or peroxide it is safe to apply immediately after the perm service.

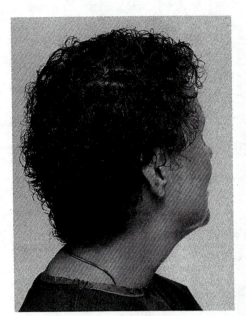

Fig. 8-22 Shape the hair to the desired length. Since the hair is reshaped every three months the length to be removed is never more than one and one-half inches. It is best to remove the length after the perm is complete.

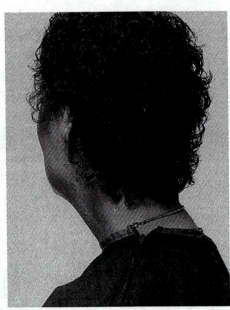

Fig. 8-23 The hair is balanced to flatter the shape of the head and project a short, yet very feminine silhouette.

"I learned through personal experience that life's trials are more easily overcome if you put up a good front. I mean that quite literally. If you look in the mirror and see an attractive person you are inclined to adjust your attitude to complement the physical appearance.

"I was an officer in the U.S. Army during World War II and was stationed in Germany. When my tour of duty was over I returned to Germany as a civilian and married a fellow officer. Before he was killed in service we were blessed with a son. I returned to the USA and remarried after 18 years.

"I occupy my spare time as a volunteer hospital worker—a member of a nationwide affiliation of 'Pink Ladies.' We are trained to communicate with families of terminally ill patients and, of course, to do all we can to make a hospital stay more pleasant for those confined to their beds. These suffering people can only judge me by my appearance and demeanor. Yes, looking physically well is very important to me."

—Natalie

natalie

Fig. 8-24 Before

Fig. 8-24A After

NATALIE: PIN CURL PERM

Technology has come full circle as far as the basic perm service is concerned. The word *perm* no longer means a head full of ringlets, expected to last for several months.

Salon professionals now offer clients a perm service that provides style support and subtle movement without full-circle curls.

The pin curl perm is a fast and effective way to create body in the hair that will hold a style through several shampoos. Because it is much less time consuming than a standard perm the price is considerably lower, making it a popular choice.

When servicing the grooming needs of maturing clients several factors must be considered other than hair texture and style preferences. For instance, consideration must be given to facial features insofar as can be visually improved by makeup or a hairstyle.

MATURE ELEGANCE

Age 55+

Name **_Natalie_**

Ch- 8

	Height	Weight	Neck	Shoulders	Face Shape	Eyes	Profile	Hair Analysis	Hair Color
4'9" – 5'									
5'2" – 5'8" +	●								
100–130 lbs.		●							
130–150+ lbs.									
Long & Thin			●						
Short									
Average									
Squared									
Rounded				●					
Humped									
Oval					●				
Square									
Round									
Pear									
Convex									
Concave									
Long nose									
Upturned nose									
Close						●			
Wide apart									
Normal							●		
Fine								●	
Coarse									
Sparse									
Dense									
Level 2–4									
Level 4–5									
Level 5–7									
Level 7–10 (gray)									●

Observation:

Hair is 100 percent gray. One eye appears smaller than the other.

Fig. 8-25

Fig. 8-26 First cut the hair to the desired length. Pin curl perms are most effective on hair lengths not exceeding three inches in the crown. Spray the hair with a mild perm solution in preparation for the "setting." Beginning approximately two inches behind the natural hairline, make stand-up pin curls with strong bases across the head.

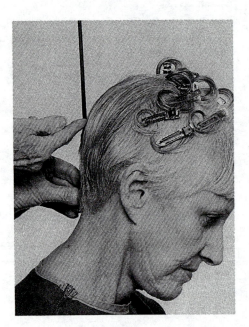

Fig. 8-27 Hold a comb against the flat of the head to determine how far down to pin curl the hair. The pin curls should extend only to the point the head curves away from the comb.

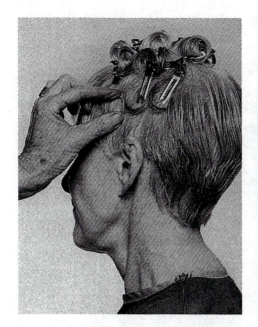

Fig. 8-28 Make flat pin curls with strong directional bases on one side of the head.

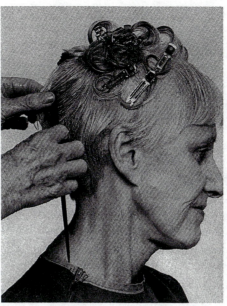

Fig. 8-29 Repeat the same flat pin curl procedure on the opposite side.

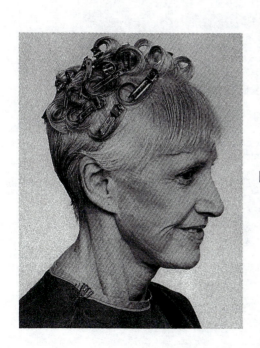

Fig. 8-30 Complete the pin curl perm by placing flat, no-volume pin curls around the stand-up curls. Form the curls in the direction in which you want the hair to move in the completed style.

NOTE:

Place a hair net over the pin curls and process as you would a standard perm. The hair is then ready to be styled.

"For thirteen years I assisted the manager and attended the desk at a prominent women's apparel store. Fashionable designer clothes and affluent, fashion-aware customers kept me conscious of my own appearance.

"I believe it is important for a woman, at any age, to stay physically fit and look her personal best. I never think of aging as a handicap. I think of it as an opportunity to exercise some choices unavailable to me in my peak productive years.

"Presently I work two days a week at an auto auction center processing invoices and keeping track of purchases. My duties require me to walk from four to six miles each day. It's a pleasant way to stay in shape.

"On a personal note, my husband and I will be celebrating our fiftieth wedding anniversary soon. We have three children, four grandchildren and four great-grandchildren. They keep us both young. I have little time for serious hobbies but I do bowl once a week. Nothing in my life will change by choice."

— Berniece

Berniece

Fig. 8-31 Before

Fig. 8-31A After

BERNIECE: SEMI-PERMANENT WAVE—
ROLLER SET PROCESSED AS A PERM

Some mature clients have beautiful, naturally gray hair that has sufficient body to hold a hairstyle for days. But for women who prefer to shampoo their own hair on a daily basis and who do not want random chemical curl (a perm), a new technique referred to as a "semi-permanent wave" is an ideal service.

The hair is set on large rollers, as if it were a temporary wet-set. The basic difference being it is processed as a standard perm. The rods are too large to break the bonds necessary for restructuring the hair. Because the hair is set in mild perm solution, processed to a weak curl formation and neutralized, it has soft movement that lasts for several weeks. The process can be repeated as often as necessary without damage to the hair.

Berniece prefers to wear her hair medium-short but sufficiently long to design a more formal style for special occasions.

The secret to keeping clients happy is to design hairstyles that make them look good. In order to do that every body feature must be taken into consideration.

MATURE ELEGANCE

Age 55+

Name **Berniece**

Ch- 8

	Height	Weight	Neck	Shoulders	Face Shape	Eyes	Profile	Hair Analysis	Hair Color
4'9" – 5'									
5'2" – 5'8" +	●								
100–130 lbs.									
130–150+ lbs.		●							
Long			●						
Short									
Average									
Squared				●					
Rounded									
Humped									
Oval									
Square									
Round					●				
Pear									
Convex									
Concave									
Long nose							●		
Upturned nose									
Close									
Wide apart									
Normal						●			
Fine								●	
Coarse									
Sparse									
Dense								●	
Level 2–4									
Level 4–5									
Level 5–7									
Level 7–10 (gray)									●

Observation:

Fig. 8-32

The Semi-Perm

Fig. 8-33 After the hair has been shampooed and towel-dried, mild perm solution is combed through one section at a time. The desired directional design is shaped into the wet hair and medium-large rollers are placed in the wave formation.

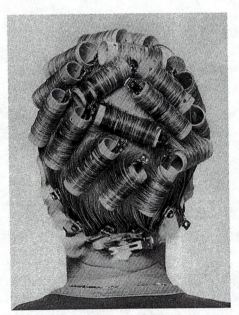

Fig. 8-34 Set the back section, angled from the tip of the left ear to the lobe of the right ear. Then complete the crown and each side. Wrap the nape hair on small standard perm rods.

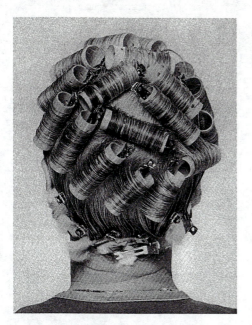

Fig. 8-35 The front is also set on the bias to create an asymmetric design.

NOTE:
....
Saturate each roller with mild perm solution, process, and neutralize as you would a standard perm. Use a hair net to hold the rollers in place. Towel-blot excess moisture from each roller and place the client under a hooded dryer.

The Comb Out

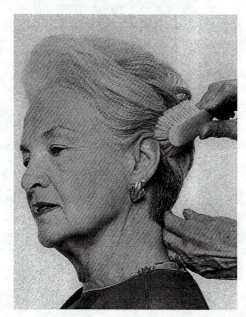

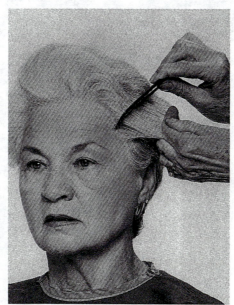

Fig. 8-36 Brush the hair thoroughly until the roller pattern blends into smooth direction.

Fig. 8-37 Lightly back-comb the hair where volume is desired and complete the hairstyle as adaptable to the client.

CHAPTER **9**

When we think of salon services we think primarily of cut, color, and perm.

Hairstyling— Various Finishing Techniques

When we think of salon services we think primarily of cut, color, and perm. There are many styling techniques that once might have been considered "quick services" that, on a daily basis, are paramount in most professional salons.

Such finishing techniques as blow-drying, Velcro and hot-roller set, iron curling, and hair extensions diversify salon services.

Ladies featured in this chapter also get all the basic services on a regular basis. To realistically represent a variety of salon services these finishing techniques were selected by the authors as information of interest to salon professionals and are therefore included in this text.

It is expected that you and your clients will find personal statements made by the ladies in this chapter very inspirational and we believe quite typical of the golden ladies referred to as "seniors."

"Staying active in a career that I love gives me all the energy and inspiration I need to stay as attractive and healthy as possible. I am treasurer of a thriving fabric retail business, one of established prestige in our community. I am a consultant to decorators and clients and am often asked to give seminars on the art and use of fabrics.

"I am very into physical fitness. I think everyone should look and feel as good as they possibly can. It's my opinion that looking good keeps you feeling young. I roller skate several times a week as well as participate in a supervised aerobics program.

"For my own pleasure I have been a runway model for many years and intend to continue as long as I am asked to do so. I feel everyone should be involved in civic awareness programs. I devote as much time as possible to the Florida Hospital Gala Club, which I find very rewarding."

—Betty

Fig. 9-1 Before

Fig. 9-1A After

BETTY: BLOW-DRYING/AIR STYLING

The hair of many clients has sufficient body and natural curl to effectively create a style by the skilled use of a blow-dryer. In order to create a style with only a blow-dryer and a round styling brush, the hair must be well shaped. Actually the shape and style is cut into the hair. The blow-dryer is used to dry the hair while direction and volume are added.

Betty's hair has been cut and colored prior to being blow-dried. The stylist shows her how to maintain her own hairstyle between salon visits. Of course she is unable to recreate the lovely styles she receives at the salon. However, the professional shaping makes it possible to keep her own hair looking good.

A blow-dryer, used as the *only* styling tool, requires professional skill. For that reason a detailed, step-by-step description follows.

While Betty is petite and has no facial features that need to be corrected, the stylist takes all her measurements into consideration when creating her hairstyle. Her statistics are shown on a personal chart. Such information is kept on file for each client.

MATURE ELEGANCE

Age 55+

Name **_Betty_**

Ch- 9

	Height	Weight	Neck	Shoulders	Face Shape	Eyes	Profile	Hair Analysis	Hair Color
4'9" – 5'									
5'2" – 5'8" +	●								
100–130 lbs.		●							
130–150+ lbs.									
Long			●						
Short									
Average									
Squared				●					
Rounded									
Humped									
Oval					●				
Square									
Round									
Pear									
Convex									
Concave									
Long nose									
Upturned nose							●		
Close									
Wide apart									
Normal						●			
Fine									
Coarse								●	
Sparse									
Dense									
Level 2–4									
Level 4–5									
Level 5–7									●
Level 7–10 (gray)									

Observation:
The hair is only 20 percent gray in the front only. High lift tint results in a lively golden blonde—slightly lighter in front for an attractive contrast.

Fig. 9-2

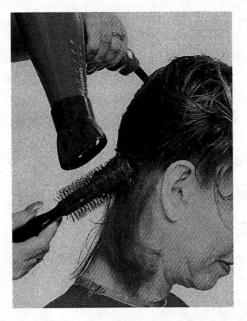

Fig. 9-3   Towel-dry the hair to a
damp stage. Part-off a
narrow section of hair in the
nape area. Use a round,
natural-bristle styling brush
and handheld blow-dryer
set on high velocity and
medium heat. Start at center
nape; pick up a narrow
panel of hair with the brush,
roll the brush toward the
ear, and direct the airflow
onto the brush.

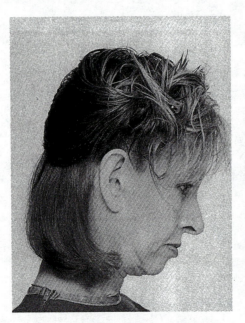

Fig. 9-4   Continue the same blow-dry
procedure, from center nape
towards each ear and up to
the top of the ears.

Fig. 9-5   Divide the back into easy-
to-handle sections. Use
the same hair-over-roller
procedure to dry and
direct the entire back.

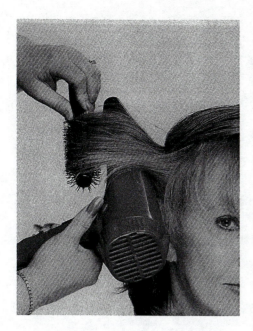

Fib. 9-6   Start picking up panels of hair on the side at the temple area. Pick up the hair with the brush and lay it over the barrel of the dryer.

Fig. 9-7   Grasp the hair with the round brush and roll it firmly toward the scalp. Direct the airflow under and over the brush until the hair wrapped around the brush is completely dry.

Fig. 9-8   Use the same drying technique until each side is completely directed and dried.

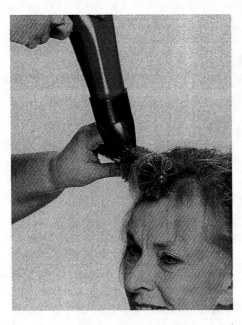

Fig. 9-9   Start at the front hairline and blow-dry the bangs and top area.

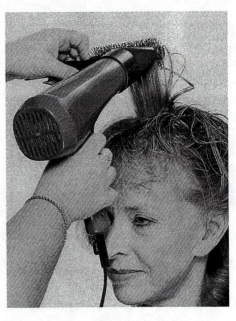

Fig. 9-10   Overdirect the hair at the scalp in the top and crown to create volume.

Fig. 9-11 When properly directed and blow-dried the hair needs no other finishing tools to create a beautiful style.

"I have never had a reason to even consider getting old. Living a long life, of course—but as far as retiring from a career I dearly love? Never!

"My college major was theatrics and communication. I began my adult career as a photographic model who, at every opportunity, worked with local theater groups. For a time I was undecided as to which media to pursue.

"For many years I have owned and actively participated in a prominent talent agency. I've had the satisfaction of seeing some of my students become supermodels and notable actresses. I feel an obligation to be an exemplary role model insofar as physical appearance is concerned. I know it is effective, for in the face of considerable competition in an area that's known as 'Hollywood East,' I am quite successful. I have always been interested in fashion and looking great. Age? Even though I am a proud grandmother, I just don't think it matters."

— Cassandra

Cassandra

Fig. 9-12 Before

Fig. 9-12A After

CASSANDRA: VELCRO ROLLER SET

Cassandra is a salon owner's ideal client inasmuch as she comes into the salon once or twice each week to keep her physical appearance representative of her professional reputation.

Setting semi-dry hair on Velcro rollers creates soft movement and volume. It is a salon service classified as "quick-service." The hair is shaped to perfection, then a blow-dryer is used to dry and direct the hair into an attractive form. Rollers that adhere to the hair without the aid of hair clips are placed in the hair as a finishing technique.

Soft or hot rollers are used almost exclusively to prepare models for photography. Since electricity is often not available to heat rollers, Velcros are the tool of choice.

Cassandra's hair is thick and in great condition. It responds easily to most setting techniques. She prefers a smooth, semi-straight style that she feels complements her facial features and looks great with minimum maintenance.

Some mature clients present no challenge to their hairstylist. Like Cassandra, they have facial features and body proportions that would be compatible with most hairstyles.

MATURE ELEGANCE
Age 55+
Name __Cassandra__
Ch- 9

	Height	Weight	Neck	Shoulders	Face Shape	Eyes	Profile	Hair Analysis	Hair Color
4'9" – 5'									
5'2" – 5'8" +	●								
100–130 lbs.		●							
130–150+ lbs.									
Long			●						
Short									
Wide									
Squared				●					
Rounded									
Humped									
Oval					●				
Square									
Round									
Normal							●		
Convex									
Concave									
Long nose									
Upturned nose									
Close									
Wide apart									
Normal						●			
Fine									
Coarse								●	
Sparse									
Dense									
Level 2–4									
Level 4–5									
Level 5–7									
Level 7–10 (gray)									●

Observation:
Very prominent eyebrows.

Fig. 9-13

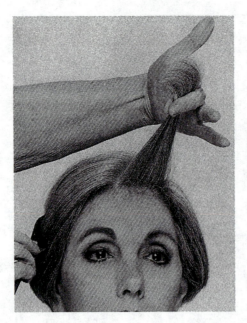

Fig. 9-14 Use the same principle when setting dry hair as you use when wet setting. For maximum lift overdirect the hair so the roller will sit half above its base.

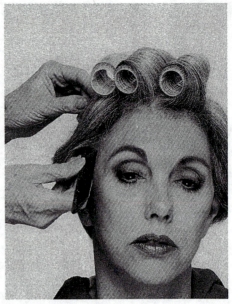

Fig. 9-15 As you work from an off-center part, progressively position each roller further off its base.

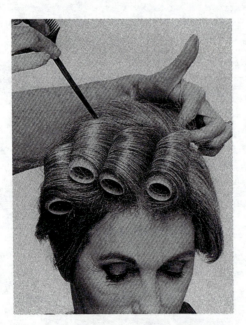

Fig. 9-16 Use neutral rollers to fill in the crown and back area. Only place rollers to the occipital bone. The nape area is graduated and fitted.

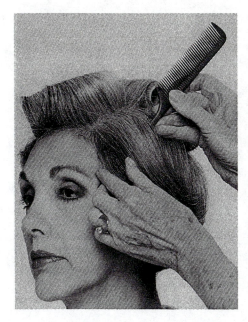

Fig. 9-17 All rollers on the opposite side are positioned to create minimum volume.

Fig. 9-18 Right side complete

Fig. 9-19 Left-side view of the completed Velcro roller set

Fig. 9-20 Back view of completed set

Fig. 9-21 A front view of the completed Velcro roller set

NOTE:
....

Place the client under a hooded dryer or use a handheld blow-dryer to thoroughly dry the hair then brush and comb the style into place. If time is not a factor the hair can be allowed to dry naturally.

"I am old-fashioned enough to believe it is bad taste to discuss a lady's age. I even go a step further and refuse even to think about it as it relates to me. I am still very active in the business world and have no intention of retiring any time soon.

"While employed as Director of Seminars and Project Development in Virginia Beach, Virginia, I was asked to plan, direct, and produce a special event being held in Orlando, Florida, for President Ronald Reagan and his lovely wife Nancy. The event was very successful and I was asked by representatives of the Orlando Science Center to remain as Director of Development. It is a very rewarding experience.

"My husband and I live in an urban home by choice. We love the cultural activities related to the inner city such as art shows and theater presentations. We take refreshing walks around beautiful Lake Eola and stroll through a multitude of informal flower gardens.

"Personal appearance is a requisite to my business position and a personal priority. I depend on my personal hairdresser to keep me looking my very best."
— MaryAnn

Fig. 9-22 Before

Fig. 9-22A After

MARYANN: IRON CURLING

The curling iron is one of the tools most often used to finish today hairstyles. The procedure is a simple one: the hair is shampooed, shaped to perfection, blowed-dry and iron-curled for volume and direction.

Most mature clients, especially those still involved in daily business activities, are regular salon clients. Many keep weekly appointments and all have their hair shaped every three to five weeks.

Busy, career clients often make appointments on a limited-time schedule, such as a lunch hour, and want the quickest service possible. Iron curling is a quick, easy, and effective way to get your client in and out of the salon in a short time.

While short hair with natural body is best suited to the iron curling procedure, the client's features and body proportions must be taken into consideration as well.

MATURE ELEGANCE
Age 55+
Name __MaryAnn__
Ch- 9

	Height	Weight	Neck	Shoulders	Face Shape	Eyes	Profile	Hair Analysis	Hair Color
4'9" – 5'									
5'2" – 5'8" +	●								
100–130 lbs.									
130–150+ lbs.		●							
Long			●						
Short									
Wide			●						
Squared									
Rounded				●					
Humped									
Oval									
Square					●				
Round									
Normal									
Convex									
Concave							●		
Long nose									
Upturned nose									
Close									
Wide apart									
Normal									
Fine									
Coarse								●	
Sparse									
Dense								●	
Level 2–4									
Level 4–5									
Level 5–7									●
Level 7–10 (gray)									

Observation:

Fig. 9-23

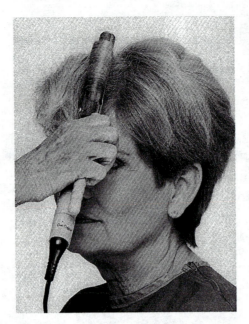

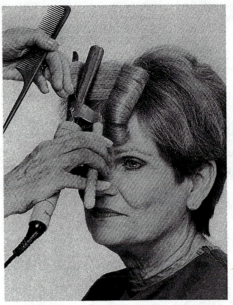

Fig. 9-24 Start at the temple area and make an on-base curl to create volume and direction. This is the lowest curl directed away from the design part.

Fig. 9-25 Continue to make barrel curls on the heavy side of the hairstyle, still directed away from the part.

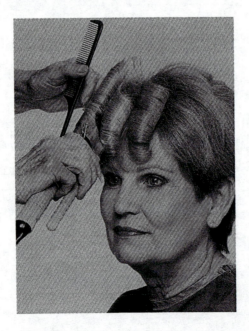

Fig. 9-26 The curl nearest the part should be overdirected to create maximum lift.

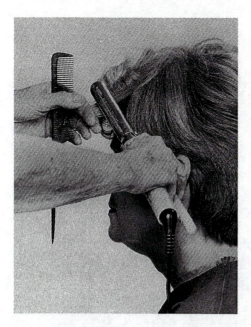

Fig. 9-27 Continue to iron-curl the heavy side and throughout the crown.

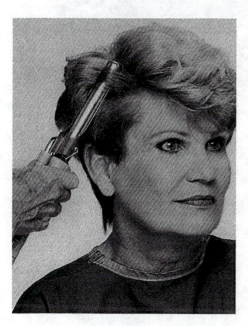

Fig. 9-28 Start at the design part on the opposite (light) side of the head. Make the first curl on base and only turn the ends from that point to the top of the ear.

NOTE:
....
Allow the hair to cool then brush and style the hair. Apply holding spray sparingly.

"I believe a woman engaged in a glamorous business must present herself at all times as a credible representative.

"I am an interior decorator with a well-established reputation for quality performance. I feel compelled to be a fashionable representative of the artistic capability of our company. Looking great at all times has its price. It means personal time spent shopping for appropriate apparel and, of course, those important visits to the hair salon. Every minute spent pays hours in dividends.

"My early years were spent in the theater circuit as a dancer. It required a lot of travel which I readily gave up to marry a great man and raise two sons. One of my sons is also an interior professional with a degree in interior design. I believe all creative arts are related and I am enjoying my second career as much as I did the first."

—Alice

Alice

Fig. 9-29 Before

Fig. 9-29A After

ALICE: HAIR ENHANCEMENT (Hair Extensions)

Women from all walks of life are discovering what Hollywood celebrities have known for ages. The secret is out! If a client's hair is thinning or simply too frail and fine to look full and luxurious just add "faux" hair wherever it is needed.

Hairstyles can go from flat to fabulous in just a few minutes. Some women who have mastered the art of adding strands or wefts of hair to their own natural locks say it is as easy as putting on lipstick.

Hair enhancers (wefts) come in a variety of natural-looking colors and many different lengths. Each item has a very small clamp at its base for easy insertion. One of the most valuable hair items is called a "circle." It is actually approximately 12 inches of hair attached on a nylon thread. Individual pieces of various lengths (12, 8, and 6 inches) are also available. One or more can be used as needed. A "circle" and one 6-inch weft were used to create a glamorous style for Alice.

Alice has excellent facial features and a body that reflects her early career as a professional dancer; however, her hair is thinning on top. Add-on hair is a real advantage to creating the styles she prefers.

MATURE ELEGANCE
Age 55+
Name _Alice_
Ch- 9

	Height	Weight	Neck	Shoulders	Face Shape	Eyes	Profile	Hair Analysis	Hair Color
4'9" – 5'									
5'2" – 5'8" +	●								
100–130 lbs.		●							
130–150+ lbs.									
Long									
Short			●						
Wide									
Squared				●					
Rounded									
Humped									
Oval					●				
Square									
Round									
Normal							●		
Convex									
Concave									
Long nose									
Upturned nose									
Close									
Wide apart									
Normal						●			
Fine								●	
Coarse									
Sparse								●	
Dense									
Level 2–4									
Level 4–5									
Level 5–7									●
Level 7–10 (gray)									

Observation:
  Hair is very thin on top.

Fig. 9-30

Preparation

Shampoo, dry, and style the hair as you normally do before adding hair enhancers. Add-on hair is meant to be used in the final styling.

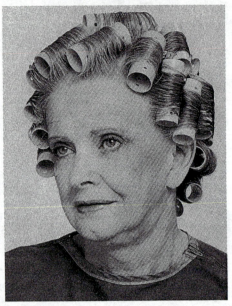

Fig. 9-31, 32, & 33   Because the hair is very fine it responds best when wet set. Use large rollers directed to create the movement desired, then place the client under a hooded dryer until the hair is completely dry.

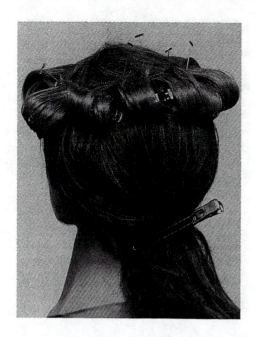

Fig. 9-34 Use T-pins to secure hair enhancers to a mannequin. Dampen the strand slightly and roll in oversized rollers. Dry the hair thoroughly before adding it to the client's own hair.

Add-On Hair Enhancers

Fig. 9-35 Remove rollers from the client's hair and the hairpieces. Brush both thoroughly. Comb the hair forward from center crown where the circle enhancer will be placed. Make a circular part completely around the head.

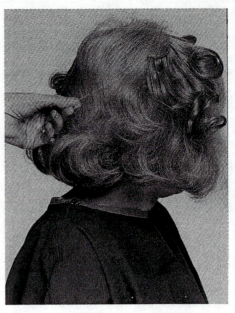

Fig. 9-36 Place the base of the circle weft of hair where the natural hair is parted.

Fig. 9-37 Secure the circle weft in the back. The nylon string may be tied or a small hairpin may be used.

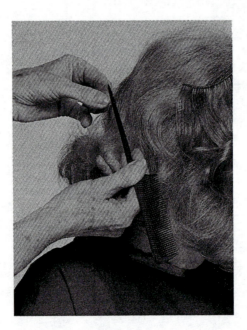

Fig. 9-38 Carefully integrate the additional hair into the hairstyle by using a rat-tail comb and a wide-bristle vent brush.

Fig. 9-39 If needed for volume, clip a 6-inch weft near the scalp in addition to the circle weft.

Fig. 9-40 The effects of the additional hair can be seen immediately.

"Looking good is one of my top priorities. It's not always easy to stay perfectly groomed as I am Den Mother to ten children. Never mind that I am not the birth mother to all of them. It's still a lot of work—rewarded by lots of love.

"I really didn't give it a second thought when I turned 55. I am too busy to let age slow me down. I work part-time as receptionist in an upscale, full-service beauty salon and do runway fashion modeling occasionally.

"If I had the time, both my major hobbies could turn into a lucrative business. I bake gourmet sweets and do intricate apparel alterations. I exercise regularly and stay as physically active as possible. Only my family is more important to me than personal appearance and physical fitness."

—Carolyn

Carolyn

Fig. 9-41 Before

Fig. 9-41A After

CAROLYN: QUICK FINISH

One of the fastest and most effective ways to put finishing touches on a terrific haircut is simply by turning the ends under with a curling iron having a medium-large barrel.

Unlike an iron-curl style, only the ends are turned under as opposed to creating volume and indentation. The hair is shampooed, cut and blow-dried. Some of the ends are well controlled; others need a little direction and control. A curling iron is the tool of choice.

Carolyn gets a soft perm approximately every three months. In between she has her hair trimmed and styled several times. When her hair needs no shaping she simply has it styled and "quick finished."

The facial features and body proportions of each client are of paramount importance when designing an adaptable hairstyle. It is even more important when servicing a mature client. She has her hair styled by a capable professional so she will look her terrific best.

MATURE ELEGANCE

Age 55+

Name **_Carolyn_**

Ch- 9

	Height	Weight	Neck	Shoulders	Face Shape	Eyes	Profile	Hair Analysis	Hair Color
4'9" – 5'									
5'2" – 5'8" +	●								
100–130 lbs.		●							
130–150+ lbs.									
Long			●						
Short									
Wide									
Squared				●					
Rounded									
Humped									
Oval					●				
Square									
Round									
Flat							●		
Convex									
Concave									
Long nose									
Upturned nose									
Close						●			
Wide apart									
Normal								●	
Fine									
Coarse									
Sparse								●	
Dense									
Level 2–4									
Level 4–5									●
Level 5–7									
Level 7–10 (gray)									

Observation:
Close set eyes, receding chin

Fig. 9-42

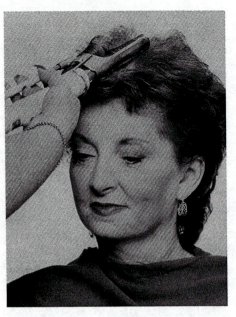

Fig. 9-43 Start turning the ends at a point slightly off center. Turn the iron until the ends are free around the barrel then give the iron only one turn to control the ends. The base of the curl is not of importance in this styling technique.

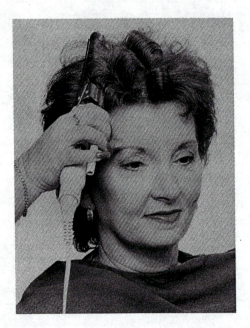

Fig. 9-44 Work in a circle from one central point until the ends of the hair in the front and crown has been turned.

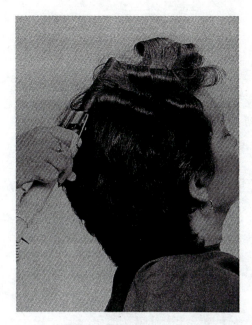

Fig. 9-45 Work from side to side over the crest of the head.

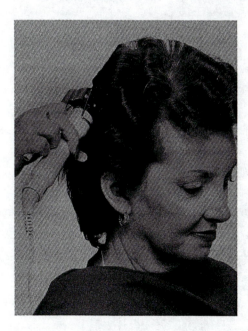

Fig. 9-46 Continue working all the way down both sides to the top of each ear and all the way down the back.

"I was born in Cuba and came to this country in 1963 to make a better life for myself and my family. Language was a barrier at first but I soon was engaged in a business where everyone spoke the language of 'fashion.' I spent eighteen years in that fascinating field.

"Success in the fashion industry begins and ends with your knowledge of the art of making others look great and—no less important—your own personal style. I developed a style with which I was comfortable. It included head-to-toe coordination, current awareness, and good taste. Nothing has changed since I retired several years ago.

"Close friends and family occupy most of my spare time. I have a son and a daughter and two grandchildren. My son works for the U.S. Government and lives in the nation's capital city. My daughter met and married a German man and is residing in that country. I am deeply proud of both of them.

"I have found, while working with the public, women who really care about personal appearance seem to have a more positive attitude about life in general and a keen sense of their own worth."

—Maria

Maria

Fig. 9-47 Before

Fig. 9-47A After

MARIA: MAKEOVER

Maria is typical of salon clients who have their hair done on a weekly schedule. The salon client who has what is called a "standing appointment" is all-but-a-vanishing breed. Make no mistake, there are still many ladies who simply do not wash their hair on a daily basis nor do they style their own hair.

Maria has her hair shaped every six weeks. She has a haircolor touch-up at the same time. In between those services she has her hair styled. The service rendered is a conditioning shampoo and rinse and iron curling.

This routine, weekly service is one of the most popular rendered in most salons. For this reason, as well as others, mature clients are of great value to a salon's effort to maintain a well-balanced clientele and a profitable cash flow.

Maria's hair is cut following the same technique used to cut the hair of Betty Jo, detailed in Chapter 7 (pages 109–113). The hair was iron-curled employing the technique used to style the hair of MaryAnn in Chapter 9 (pages 158-161).

MATURE ELEGANCE

Age 55+

Name ___Maria___

Ch· 9

	Height	Weight	Neck	Shoulders	Face Shape	Eyes	Profile	Hair Analysis	Hair Color
4'9" – 5'									
5'2" – 5'8" +	●								
100–130 lbs.									
130–150+ lbs.		●							
Long									
Short			●						
Wide			●						
Squared									
Rounded				●					
Humped									
Oval									
Square									
Round					●				
Normal							●		
Convex									
Concave									
Long nose									
Upturned nose									
Close						●			
Wide apart									
Normal								●	
Fine									
Coarse									
Sparse									
Dense									
Level 2–4									
Level 4–5									●
Level 5–7									
Level 7–10 (gray)									

Observation:
 70 percent gray, very pointed chin

Fig. 9-48

NOTES

NOTES

NOTES

NOTES

NOTES

NOTES